I0830017

Cognitive Behavioral Therapy

The Ultimate Guide to Using CBT to Rewire Your Brain and Overcoming Anxiety, Depression, Phobias, PTSD, Compulsive Behavior, and Anger, Including DBT and ACT Techniques

Contents

Introduction

Cognitive behavioral therapy (CBT) is fast becoming one of the most sought methods of treatment for a variety of health complications, particularly mental and emotional health problems. The National Center for Biotechnology Information conducted research into the efficacy of cognitive behavioral therapy, and they found that not only did the treatment allay symptoms of various illnesses, but the results of the treatment were long-lasting! More people are testing the curative powers of CBT by the day, and this has created a demand for CBT therapists.

The purpose of this book is to provide a comprehensive look at what CBT entails. The book explores the various tools and techniques used in CBT therapy, how CBT can help people fighting against various mental illnesses, and the role of CBT in creating a perfectly balanced life.

CBT emphasizes a hands-on approach to problems; whereby the therapist helps the client comprehend the intricate web of their thoughts, emotions, and behaviors. The underlying philosophy of CBT is that before you can change a person's emotions or behaviors, you first have to change their thoughts.

For the success of CBT, a therapist and a client must get along and have a deep trust between one another. The goal is to break the cycle of unhelpful thought patterns.

Chapter 1: What is Cognitive Behavioral Therapy?

Cognitive behavioral therapy (CBT) is a form of psychotherapy that solves an individual's problems by helping them modify both their thoughts and actions. CBT takes on a practical approach toward solving problems. Its goal is to remedy toxic thought-patterns and behaviors that have contributed to a person's distress and thus restore happiness. CBT is commonly used in treating a number of problems, such as relationship issues, sleeping difficulties, drug abuse, anxiety, and depression.

One of the biggest advantages of CBT is its shortness. It takes about six to ten months for the treatment of most emotional problems. Clients attend weekly sessions or a session every two weeks, with each session lasting about an hour. During the session, the client bares their soul, and the therapist comes up with the strategies of solving the problem. The therapist introduces a set of principles to the patient. And these lifelong principles are to help the patient overcome their problems.

Psychologists consider CBT to be a blend of psychotherapy and behavioral therapy. Psychotherapy highlights the value of the personal meanings we ascribe to things and how thinking patterns start in early childhood. Behavioral therapy explores the connection between our challenges, behaviors, and thoughts. To achieve maximum results, psychotherapists must tailor CBT to the precise needs and character of every patient.

The History of Cognitive Behavioral Therapy

Aaron Beck, a psychiatrist, is the man that came up with cognitive behavioral therapy in the 1960s. During psychoanalysis, Aaron realized that some of his patients appeared to talk to themselves, a sign of internal dialogue, but the patients only reported a small part of these thoughts to him.

For instance, during therapy, the patient might think to herself, *The therapist seems a bit cold today. Have I done something to annoy him?* Such a line of thought could make the patient anxious. But then the patient says to herself, *Maybe he's tired, or he had a terrible encounter with someone before coming here.* The second thought would potentially make the patient go from anxious to comfortable and well-adjusted. Thus, by changing their thoughts, they get to change their feelings.

Aaron Beck found out that the connection between thoughts and feelings was crucial. He said that people weren't always conscious of their emotion-filled thoughts, but they could be trained to recognize them. Beck thought that it was necessary for a person to identify their emotion-filled thoughts in order to remedy their problems.

The Place of Negative Thoughts

According to CBT, whatever happens to us is not liable for our frustrations, but the meaning that we ascribe to it. If something terrible goes down, it is the accompanying negative thoughts that will make us feel terrible, not the deed itself.

For example, if a woman is suffering from depression, she might think to herself, *If I go to work today, I'll botch things up. I feel horrible.* Because of believing her negative thoughts, she is going to call in sick and miss work. She's the victim of her thoughts – not her depression. She made an incorrect assumption. Maybe if she'd gone to work, she'd have found something to do and proceeded to be extremely productive. However, sitting at home for the whole day, the negativity increases tenfold, and she's thinking, *Oh, I'm such a letdown! Where do I go from here?* The woman ends up feeling even worse than before. Her emotion-filled thoughts place her in a vicious cycle that sends her spiraling down into a continuously worse state.

Where Do These Negative Thoughts Come From?

According to Aaron Beck, the most negative thinking patterns are rooted in our childhood experiences. A child who never received parental love might grow up to want validation from the external world. For this, they will strive to do something extraordinary to capture everyone's attention and bask in the validation that they will earn. But this might place the person in a situation known as a dysfunctional assumption. This is where a previously unloved person assumes that they always have to do something great in order to be loved by people, and this notion makes them pursue success relentlessly, yet when they experience failure, the dysfunctional assumption is activated, and they start perceiving themselves as failures who will never recover.

Cognitive behavioral therapy is geared at helping patients understand the role of their negative thoughts in their distressing lives. Patients can recognize their automatic thoughts and test their validity. For instance, in the case of the depressed woman, instead of thinking at once that she won't cope at work, she should have prodded for reasons that support the opposite.

CBT Treatment

The difference between cognitive behavioral therapy and other forms of psychotherapies is that CBT sessions are structured, and purposely discourage patients from having a multidimensional talk. At the start, the patient meets the therapist to divulge their specific challenges. The therapist sets goals that the patient must achieve within a certain time frame. The problems are varied in nature: sleeping troubles, difficulties in socializing, lack of concentration, or even unhappy marriage.

The challenges and the goals form the basis of the session structures. During each session, the therapist and the patient will jointly agree on the milestone they have to reach. The sessions have to be structured in a progressive way, with the easy parts tackled before the difficult ones. At the end of each session, there has to be an assignment to be performed before the next session.

Who Can Be Helped By CBT?

CBT is most effective when there are clear goals. For this reason, people with specific challenges are the most suitable for CBT treatment. People with vague feelings and who have no particular aspect of their lives that they want to develop will not achieve great results with CBT.

CBT can help solve the following issues:

- Anger issues
- Anxiety
- Panic attacks
- Chronic fatigue syndrome
- Chronic pain
- Depression
- Alcoholism
- Bulimia nervosa
- Mood swings
- Obsessive-compulsive disorder
- Phobias
- Insomnia

Chapter 2: A Step-by-Step Guide to CBT

Cognitive behavioral therapy helps to alleviate various problems by providing a short, goal-oriented, and problem-specific approach. The success of CBT hinges upon the active involvement of the patient. The therapist and the patient jointly write down the goals that they should achieve within a certain time frame. In the beginning, the patient must work alongside the therapist, but ultimately, the patient could become their own therapist.

- First off, the patient must scout for a therapist that they are comfortable working with.
- If the patient lucks out to find the best therapist, an appointment is set up.
- During the first appointment, the patient will divulge every last detail about their problems, with the therapist asking necessary questions.
- The therapist is to draft a set of milestones to be achieved within a certain amount of time.
- Then the therapist will come up with a structured CBT course that will help the patient realize the set milestones.
- The patient is expected to attend sessions over the next few months until they achieve their goals.

Beliefs that CBT is based upon

- *Unhelpful ways that people think can lead to mental and emotional problems:* At the root of our challenges, is a complex web of unhelpful thoughts. These negative thinking patterns not only hinder us from having clarity of thought but also give way to harmful behaviors. For instance, if a college student becomes a young mother, it is so easy for her to abandon the dreams she had and focus on being a mother. However, if she can view her condition from the angle of positivity, she will continue pursuing her goals despite the fact that she has a child.

- *If people learn toxic behaviors, this too can lead to mental and emotional problems:* For the most part, a toxic behavior is acquired from negative associations. If a young man starts hanging out with the wrong crowd, he will become influenced negatively. The crowd might make him smoke cigarettes, consume alcohol, and get involved in reckless sexual behavior. These kinds of behaviors would erode his sense of morality and convert him into a decadent young man. Toxic behaviors are like cancer – they spread out to all the parts. Thus, the person will start having troubles in his relationships, finances, spirituality, and work environment.

- *People can learn more helpful ways of thinking and behaving*: It's all about awareness and making a commitment. The helpful ways of thinking and behaving are not alien to us. We have many models that we can cope from. If we apply ourselves, we can modify both our thoughts and behaviors. Learning great behaviors is about consuming the right information and keeping the right associations. Ensure that you keep company with positive people so that you may copy their positivity. Also, ensure that you feed your mind with positivity, so that your emotions may stabilize.

• Fresh habits can allay symptoms of mental and physical conditions and allow people to behave in better ways: Innovation is at the heart of the advancement of a human being. When you create new routines and take on new habits, you reduce the potency of your mental and physical issues and increase your capacity to be more grounded. You acquire new habits by being an interesting person and developing your strengths. If you focus on improving your skills and capabilities, you stimulate your creative mind in the process. This is likely to lead you into new habits that you never thought possible.

The therapist and the patient must work together in order to reach the set milestones.

CBT can help the Patient Learn the Following:

• Identify problems more clearly: Through the various principles set down by the therapist, a patient is in a position to understand the true nature of their problems. Some feelings may have a sense of ambiguity so that the problem becomes two-faced. But CBT helps you understand precisely what ails you and how you can restore your health.

• Become aware of automatic thoughts: Aaron Beck argued that automatic thoughts influence most of our thinking patterns and behaviors. These automatic thoughts are basically emotion-filled thoughts. They are rooted in our early childhood, and it is difficult to be conscious of them. Recognizing automatic thoughts is a big step toward solving your problems.

• Challenge untrue assumptions: For most people battling mental health issues, holding untrue assumptions is the norm. For instance, they might think that no one loves them, they are ugly, or they are not good enough. All of these assumptions can be challenged and proven to

be erroneous. This helps them get started on the path to recovery.

• *Differentiate facts from myths:* We live in an era where myths tend to be perpetuated at the expense of facts. This causes people to be extremely sensitive to their plight. However, through CBT, a person can tell apart the truth from deception. This empowers them to make appropriate decisions.

• *Understand how the past affects the present*: If you had a nasty childhood experience, it most likely scarred you and the effects are noticeable to this day. For instance, you may be prone to catching panic attacks or developing anxiety whenever your mind calls back the memories of your early childhood.

The Advantages of CBT

CBT has been proven to be extremely effective in the treatment of stress-related conditions and anxiety. The following are some of the advantages of CBT:

> • *Time-saving:* CBT doesn't take long to complete as compared to other talk therapies. People with mental and emotional ailments favor taking CBT because it is both short and effective. As long as the therapist and the patient get along, then it becomes easy to reach the set milestones.
>
> • *Focuses on modifying your thoughts and behaviors:* The main philosophy of CBT is that a person's thought patterns and behaviors are responsible for their feelings. So CBT takes on a practical approach to modify the thoughts and behaviors of a person, and, as a result, improve their feelings.

CBT principles are very useful: The set of principles and skills that a therapist hands down to the patient are extremely helpful in day-to-day living. They can be applied in every phase of life. These skills help a person to become all-around developed and better at overcoming various life difficulties.

Chapter 3: CBT Tools and Techniques

There are many tools and techniques employed in cognitive behavioral therapy, and many of these tools and techniques have been incorporated into day-to-day living. The following are some of the efficient and regularly used tools and techniques in CBT:

Journaling

During the day, we experience many moods and thoughts that often escape our attention. Through journaling, you can capture these moods and thoughts, and in addition, you may specify the time, the source, the extent or intensity, and your response. When you unravel your thought patterns and emotional behaviors, it becomes far easier to modify the negative parts about you. Although journaling is traditionally a CBT technique, it is widely adopted in everyday living. Many people have taken to writing down their moods and emotions of the day, and this helps them understand themselves much better. Journaling helps you keep track of your development.

Unraveling Cognitive Distortions

Cognitive distortions are erroneous thinking patterns that subject us to a faulty reality. It is simply a case of your brain lying to you. The brain is your biggest ally. It shields you from danger, tells you of potential mates, and keeps you aware of your surroundings. But there are moments that you have to distrust what your brain tells you, simply because it has relied upon the wrong signals. The brain is always linking up thoughts with ideas and behaviors. It is necessary to become aware of instances where the brain has made erroneous connections.

Cognitive Restructuring

Identifying your cognitive distortions and the fallacies you hold is merely half of the challenge. The other half is to explore the origins of your cognitive distortions and how you came to believe the fallacies. This will help you get rid of erroneous beliefs and fallacies. For instance, if you strongly believe that you must have a perfect look in order to attract members of the opposite sex, and then by some stroke of misfortune you lose your looks, you are going to feel terribly bad about yourself. Instead of hanging on this obviously flawed belief, you might want to learn the deepest factors that draw people in.

Exposure and Response Prevention

If you have a certain weakness, your first instinct might be to run away from it. You imagine that the more you distance yourself from a weakness, the safer you are. However, that's incorrect. You can get rid of a weakness by overexposing yourself to it. For instance, if you have a porn addiction, don't block all porn websites. Instead, make all the websites available, but grow your willpower so that you're not tempted to click on a porn website. This technique is effective for people with obsessive-compulsive disorder. It achieves major results when used in combination with journaling.

Interoceptive Exposure

This technique is for people with panic attacks and anxiety. It involves exposing a person to stimuli to activate their fears. There must be no distractions or avoidance. The objective is to make the sufferer realize that panic symptoms are not harmful. The sufferer is in a position to overcome their fears after extended exposure to stimuli. For instance, if you become overwhelmed with anxiety while in a dark room, the answer is not to shun dark rooms. You should stay in a dark room, let all your usual responses kick into action, and endure the nasty feeling altogether. In the end, you get to realize that there's nothing to fear.

Nightmare Exposure and Rescripting

This technique is for people who battle nightmares. It is very similar to interoceptive exposure. The scenario is set up in a manner to awaken the person's nightmares. Then, the patient and therapist work together to identify the emotion that they desire and develop a concept or image for accompanying that emotion. Ultimately, the affected person gets to overcome their nightmare by developing an alternative mental image. To pull through this technique, there have to be strong collaborative skills from the therapist and the patient, a fertile imagination, and some consistency.

Play the Script to the End

This is another technique designed for the sufferers of fear and anxiety. In this technique, a person with the tendency of being fearful and anxious gets to conduct a thought experiment, in which they imagine the worst possible outcome of their fears. Letting yourself imagine the extreme makes you realize that you can endure everything. This mindset delivers the sufferer from their bondage of fear. For instance, if you are terribly anxious about talking to a member of the opposite sex, letting yourself imagine getting rejected will eliminate the fear factor. You realize that you will do just fine beyond the rejection.

Progressive Muscle Relaxation

This technique is about relaxing one muscle group at a time until your full body attains a state of relaxation. You typically begin from the head and move down to the toes. For the best results, apply a bit of pressure to your muscles and also incorporate audio or video guidance. This technique is incredibly useful for calming nerves and restoring your focus. Also, it helps to be consistent.

Relaxed Breathing

This technique is aimed at bringing calmness and regularity to your breathing. You can practice relaxed breathing with the help of audio and videos or your own imagination. When you reach a balanced state, you are in a position to tackle your problems with unmatched rationality. The best tip for practicing relaxed breathing is finding a serene environment.

Chapter 4: Automatic and Intrusive Thoughts

The architect of cognitive behavioral therapy, Aaron Beck, emphasized that automatic thoughts play a huge role in our feelings. Automatic thoughts are merely emotion-filled thoughts that are elicited by a trigger such as an event or an action. They are called automatic because you have no conscious knowledge of them taking place.

Automatic thoughts can be advantageous. For instance, you might be driving and then it starts raining heavily. An automatic thought will pop into your mind, *Please be careful!* This will cause you to be anxious and drive with much caution.

Sadly, automatic thoughts can be the bearers of negativity, especially for people who struggle with mental and emotional health issues. For instance, an anxious person might see a frowning person looking in their direction, and they will automatically think, *That person hates me!* This will cause them to worry and feel sad needlessly, and they couldn't be further from the truth, considering that the frowning person might just be battling stomach pains.

Cognitive behavioral therapy is concerned with unraveling the automatic thoughts that contribute to negativity in an individual's mind. Once a person understands their automatic thoughts, they are empowered to get rid of their negativity.

The underlying philosophy of cognitive behavioral therapy is that thoughts, feelings, and behaviors are entangled in a multifaceted camaraderie. Considering the huge role that thoughts play in shaping our feelings and behaviors, we have to alter our thought patterns if we are to modify our feelings or behaviors.

The ABC Model of Emotions

A: **Event:** Boyfriend doesn't pick up your call.

B: **<u>Thought:</u>** *This is awful! My boyfriend is mad at me! Maybe he wants to dump me!*

C: **<u>Feelings:</u>** Anxiety takes over. The heart knocks on your chest. You get stressed.

We have all experienced an event that triggered a negative thinking pattern. However, as much as we cannot control the things that happen, we can control how we respond to them.

Characteristic of Negative Automatic Thoughts

- *Short and simple:* An automatic thought is expressed in short phrases. This creates more impact. For instance, if you're driving at night and your headlights die out, you will automatically think, *I'm in trouble!* and not something like, *Now the headlights are dead, and I have about 30 miles to cover!*
- *Always believed:* Automatic thoughts pop into our minds, and we believe them at once. We never stop to question their validity. For this reason, automatic thoughts are very powerful. If you are to overcome your negative thought pattern, you surely have to challenge the authenticity of your automatic thoughts.

They worsen the situation: An automatic thought rides on the wings of fear. When an automatic thought pops into your mind, the dreadfulness goes up. For instance, if you were driving in a lonely part of the road at night and your car dies down, at first you will become afraid, and then anxious, and then panic attacks. The fear factor builds up.   The difference between automatic thoughts and intrusive thoughts is that automatic thoughts at least have a trigger. Intrusive thoughts pop into your mind out of thin air.

Intrusive thoughts pop into your mind without any warning, and their nature is often alarming or disturbing. Almost everyone finds themselves having intrusive thoughts. However, some people have a difficult time pushing away these thoughts once they appear.

What Causes Intrusive Thoughts?

Some psychologists believe that when an intrusive thought appears in a recurring fashion, it indicates that there's a problem touching upon the subject. For instance, if you keep receiving intrusive thoughts that depict naked people having sex, perhaps it's your mind trying to get you to look for sex.

Although the scientific world has no real evidence to point to the origin of intrusive thoughts, another big concern is their sticky nature. For constant sufferers of intrusive thoughts, it can be hard to get rid of them. It doesn't matter whether you choose to ignore them or not, they just keep hanging in the back of your mind until you pay them attention.

If you find yourself having to deal with violent, degrading or strange intrusive thoughts on a regular basis, then you are facing a major mental health issue. The two most common disorders associated with intrusive thoughts are anxiety and obsessive-compulsive disorder. Additionally, intrusive thoughts may be indicative of depression, Post-Traumatic Stress Disorder, Bipolar Disorder, and Attention Deficit-Hyperactivity Disorder.

Having the occasional intrusive thought is totally normal. However, if you experience recurring intrusive thoughts or you get stuck on your intrusive thoughts, you may be suffering from a mental or emotional health issue.

Intrusive Thoughts and Anxiety

People battling anxiety have to struggle with unwanted thoughts popping into their mind. Sometimes, your intrusive thoughts may be informed by the nature of your anxiety. For instance, people with generalized anxiety have a tendency of receiving intrusive thoughts involving one of their loved ones, whereas, people with social phobias tend to receive intrusive thoughts that remind them of a moment they embarrassed themselves.

Intrusive Thoughts and OCD

Every sufferer of obsessive-compulsive disorder battles a severe form of intrusive thoughts. It leads to the sufferer having a negative evaluation of thoughts. This is basically a person thinking that something is wrong with them for having such intrusive thoughts. People with OCD are extremely distressed about intrusive thoughts, and in their bid to get rid of these thoughts, they fall into an even worse state.

Intrusive Thoughts and Depression

Repetitive, intrusive thoughts often lead to depression. And this is especially the case when the thoughts are of a depressing nature. The following are some of the intrusive thoughts a depressed person might have:

- o Extreme self-evaluation
- o Always expecting the worst
- o Ruminating over a potentially negative outcome
- o Overthinking
- o Mind-reading others
- o Creating hills out of anthills
- o Always assuming the worst

Chapter 5: How to Set Goals Using CBT

Most of the time, we want to change our lives for the better, but for some reason, we have no idea where to start. Goal setting is one of the ingenious ways of changing your life for the better. It allows you to take notice of your weaknesses and capitalize on your strengths. The following are some of the steps you need to take in order to achieve your goals:

Step One: Identify Your Goals

Goals are critical for the achievement of success. You have to set goals and work hard to achieve these goals. Most people who have achieved success didn't go about it anyhow way; they put in place goals that kept them focused. Similarly, you have to set a goal and go for it. There are three main categories for goals: short term, medium term, and long term. Short-term goals are the goals you want to fulfill as soon as possible, medium term are those that you want to fulfill within a reasonably long amount of time, whereas, long-term goals are the things you want to accomplish in the far future.

Goals are especially helpful in the following areas:

o Relationship

o Career

o Finances

o Health

o Lifestyle

o Personal development

Qualities of Good Goals:

- *They should be realistic:* Make sure that you know the difference between realistic goals and unreachable goals. If you have unrealistic goals, you are only inflicting needless pain on yourself. Also, setting unreachable goals is indicative of an inability to manage your life, as well as being in touch with reality. To set a realistic goal, you have to identify your skill set and then find out the precise thing that you want to achieve. For instance, if you're a good fiction writer, your goals can be centered on writing a book and selling a certain amount of copies through a traditional publisher and online platforms.

- *They should be concrete and specific:* When setting goals, some people tend to be incredibly cavalier. They seem to have very vague goals, and it comes off as if they aren't sure of what they want. Your chances of achieving a goal increase when you make a goal concrete and specific. This allows you to channel all your energies on achieving a certain goal instead of taking guesses or expecting a miracle. Closing in on a specific goal is advantageous because it promotes appropriate utilization of resources. For instance, if you plan to lose weight through exercise, it is not enough to just say write down "exercise" as one of your goals. You must state the kinds of exercises you will focus on, and the time you will devote to each form of exercise.

Step Two: Break Goals into Smaller Steps

In the case of medium-term and long-term goals, you may break down your goals into smaller steps. This will quicken the realization of your goals. For instance, if one of your long-term goals is to achieve financial freedom, ensure that you put away a certain amount of money in a savings account every month, as well as starting businesses annually. When you break down your goals, it becomes easier to get more stuff done. You have a lot more energy to expand, and more importantly, you get into the right headspace necessary for achieving your goals.

Step Three: Identify Your Obstacles

It doesn't matter what we do, but there will always be obstacles in every phase of our lives. When setting goals, you want to have knowledge of various obstacles on your path. For instance, if one of your goals is to attend the gym each evening, it means you will be spending less time with your family. It is upon you to navigate this sensitive issue so that in the end, you achieve your body goals but not at the expense of your relationships. For instance, you could make up for the time lost while at the gym by taking your loved ones out on a regular basis or settling for a compromise that works for both of you.

Step Four: Schedule Your Activities

You are in a much better position of fulfilling your goals if you are clear about your actions. This will eliminate confusion and promote hard work. For instance, if your goal is to achieve a great body by attending the gym, you have to be concise about the activities you will perform. Instead of just going to the gym, schedule your warm-ups, workouts, and downtimes. The more you operate on a schedule, the more you make great use of your time. In the race toward goal achievement, time is of the essence.

Step Five: Be Diligent

The simple truth is that success is never handed to you on a silver platter. You have to strive to achieve your goals. If you would like to eliminate the struggle, you have to develop a system that promotes self-motivation. You might also want to incorporate strategies that will keep you disciplined. Don't look at it with an all-or-nothing attitude; instead, learn to be flexible. The biggest secret to diligence is consistency. Stick to your schedules regardless of what you're going through and eventually, you will achieve your goals. It helps to keep a positive attitude too.

Chapter 6: How to Use Behavioral Activation to Overcome Anxiety and Depression

Behavior activation is one of the major goals of cognitive behavioral therapy. Behavioral activation is geared at helping patients indulge in enjoyable activities and improve their problem-solving skills. A major consequence of depression is the loss of interest in activities you once found enjoyable. A depressed person will stop caring about the things they once enjoyed because they consider them unhelpful.

Shunning the things you once enjoyed worsens depression, instead of making things any better. Through behavioral activation, the therapist helps the patient let themselves go, as they indulge in enjoyable activities, and the presence of other people makes it even much more enjoyable. Apart from having fun, behavioral activation is also critical in eliminating obstacles, particularly the mental and emotional obstacles.

A patient should keep track of how this experience affects them. If the projected results are not realized, then the patient is at liberty to explore new ways of achieving the desired effect. To a great extent, the success of CBT depends on the cooperation and enthusiasm of the patient.

Our Actions Affect How We Feel

There is a great correlation between how we act and how we end up feeling. Actions that we deem great bring us joy, whereas actions that we deem inappropriate bring us grief. If we engage in activities that we value, we get rewarded with happiness and contentment. For instance, if you attach a lot of importance to socializing, you will always be in high spirits during social events because you are doing something that you consider valuable.

However, when a person gets depressed, they start losing a taste for the things that they once enjoyed. They stop caring about the things they once loved simply because it won't take away their depression. For instance, if they had been big on socializing, they now withdraw from the social scene and start exhibiting reclusive tendencies.

The worst form of depression leads the affected person into isolation and apathy. Consequently, the person misses out on opportunities for getting ahead in life or having fun.

Behavioral activation challenges the depressed person to drop their negative attitude and start engaging in the activities they once valued. The more they engage in these activities, hopefully, the faster their sense of pride and self-worth will come back.

Steps of Behavioral Activation:

Step one: Activity and Mood Monitoring

When a person gets severely depressed, they lose touch with their mood changes. Their moods obviously experience oscillations, but the depressed person perceives everything as dark. Behavioral activation helps the patient keep track of their mood changes. The patient is to write down both the activities that they engage in and then rate their depression. Additionally, they are to watch for changes in moods.

Step Two: The Relationship between Particular Activities and Moods

With enough recording of the activities and the accompanying moods, the patient can determine the particular activities that boost their moods, and the activities that put them in a worse condition.

Step Three: Focus on Activities That Improve Moods

With the help of a therapist, a patient is to single out the activities that have elicited a great mood and focus on them. The end goal is to ensure that all negativity is banished, and the first step toward achieving this is to boost the patient's moods.

Step Four: Balance Pleasure and Achievement-Based Activities

Some of the activities you are involved in produce pleasure; for instance, dancing and socializing. But other activities may not be as pleasurable but will give you a sense of achievement; for instance, attending work or cleaning your apartment. To get the best of both worlds, you have to strike a balance between the activities that give you pleasure and the activities that grant you a sense of achievement.

Step Five: Action before Motivation

The patient must do what is expected of them at all times. If there's an activity in their diary, then they must do it. Depression tends to stop a person from taking any action. However, this is limiting considering that action has to be taken before anxiety and depression are gotten rid of. If the activity proves too challenging, the patient should look for something doable that will still help their agenda of improving their moods and getting rid of their depression.

Step 6: Reward Yourself

If you manage to pull through the activities, then you deserve to reward yourself. Handling depression is akin to getting hold of a hot potato; it is extremely challenging. If you have managed to overcome the voices in your mind discouraging you from performing the mood-boosting activities, give yourself a treat.

Behavioral activation might seem like a simple coping skill, but it can be incredibly challenging to pull through the activities, especially if you lack self-motivation. The following are some tips to lighten the activities found in behavioral activation:

Identify Activities that are uniquely important to you

For maximum effectiveness of behavioral activation, a patient has to find activities that are important to them. A patient must not follow trends blindly or copy what others are doing. They should identify the activities that are important to them. In this way, they will be sufficiently self-motivated.

Have specific activities and measure progress

Your activities should be both precise and measurable. There's a greater chance of fulfilling an activity if it's specific rather vague. For instance, instead of embarking on "socializing", you should instead make it specific, "asking women out on dates". When your activity is specific, you can quantify your results much better.

Arrange your activities from easiest to hardest

An anxious or depressed person is not exactly the most self-motivated person. Knowing this, you should rank your list of activities from the easiest to the hardest. You are much more likely to get started on something if it's relatively easy than if it were difficult.

Chapter 7: How to Identify and Change Negative Thought Patterns with CBT

Many people are plagued with the plight of negative thoughts. Having negative thoughts impacts both emotions and behaviors. To improve our quality of life, it is necessary to counter these negative thoughts. This is doable through identifying negative thinking patterns and altering your thoughts.

Identifying Negative Thought Patterns

Our thoughts are interconnected with our feelings and behaviors. The way we think affects both how we feel and act. The first step toward recovering from negativity is identifying various negative thinking patterns. When you take note of your negative thoughts, you get a better understanding of your mind and emotions and are in a much better position to develop positive thoughts.

Some types of negative thoughts include, *I'm so stupid, I'm so foolish,* and, *I'm unlucky.*

If you find it difficult to be introspective and admit to your negative thoughts, you should ask a trusted friend or family member to keep track of your negative ways of thought.

Find Out the Causes of Your Negative Thought Patterns

The next challenge is to identify the sources of your negative thoughts. For instance, if one of your negative thoughts is, *I'm ugly, no one likes me!* try to understand the action or event that triggered this thought. Being good at identifying the causes of our negative thoughts calls us to be introspective. Maybe the source of your negative thought is your childhood abuse. If a close family member told you that you are not beautiful, you might have taken it to heart, and have been since looking for evidence to support your flawed belief. A member of the opposite sex might look at you with a frown – for other reasons of course – but you will still deduct from their facial expression that they find you ugly.

Highlight Unhelpful Thought Patterns

It is one thing having negative thought patterns, and it is another having unhelpful thought patterns. These are also known as core beliefs. The unhelpful thought patterns are ingrained into a person's psyche. Unhelpful thought patterns tend to be divorced from reality. For instance, if you have been telling yourself, "I'm stupid," for long enough, it will cease being just a negative thought and graduate into a core belief. This will lead you to automatically shunning opportunities and people that you consider too smart for you.

List down the Consequences of Your Negative Thoughts

To be more involved in actively changing your negative thought patterns, you have to identify the consequences that you suffer. For instance, if your negative thought, *I'm foolish* causes you to detach yourself from your peers or stops you from going for the opportunities that you deserve, take note of these consequences so that you may increase your resolve to change your situation. At one point, you will have had enough and decide that you want to change.

You may also list down past negative experiences and consequences that occurred as a result of negative thinking patterns.

Keep a Record of Your Thoughts

Using a worksheet, track the number of negative thoughts that you experience on a daily or weekly basis. Also, note down the ideas that support a thought and the ideas that do not support a thought. For instance, if one of your negative thoughts is, *I'm a loser,* ideas that do not support this negative thought include, "I'm a great person", "I have a sharp mind", and "I don't need everyone to like me!" Try to determine the days during which you experience low cases of negative thought patterns and the days when the negativity shoots through the roof.

Avoid Negative Language

Create a list of negative words that you use often. For instance, "can't" and "won't", and make a conscious decision of using more balanced words like "sometimes" or "most of the time". When you have a negative way of thinking, it affects even the language you use. But you must make a conscious effort to alter this situation. By developing a language that promotes positivity, you will be sending a message to your brain to challenge its negative thinking patterns.

Explore the Connection between Your Emotions and Negative Thoughts

Whenever you experience a negative emotion, start by questioning the thought behind it. For instance, if you get anxious or depressed, go back to the thought that you just had. You will find that the thought was depressive in nature. For instance, you might have wondered why you have taken so long to achieve success or why you haven't settled, or you might have just thought that you're not good enough. Always monitor your thoughts and take notice of the negative thoughts. When you catch a negative thought early enough, it is easy to amend it. For example, instead of thinking, *I'm not good enough* by means of a mantra, you want to think, *I'm a great person!*

Choose Positive Explanations

No matter how your actions appear conventionally terrible, you can always rationalize them. For instance, if you had a child while you're still young, instead of looking at it as throwing your dreams away, look at it as bringing something new into the world. The same case applies to your thoughts. On the occasions that you experience negative thoughts, you want to find a positive or realistic explanation.

List down the Things That You're Grateful For

When you are battling negative thoughts, it is quite easy to overlook the many positive things about your life. To shift your mindset from negativity into positivity, you have to list down the things that you are grateful for. Some of the things that you ought to be grateful for include family, lovers, pets, and home. Whenever you fall short of your expectations, think about what you already have, and close the door to negative thinking patterns.

Practice Mindfulness

Instead of getting lost in the negative thoughts roaring in your mind, learn to shift your focus to the present. Pay direct attention to the things that you are doing at that moment, such as eating, drinking, and other daily activities.

Seek Guidance and Support

Don't bury yourself in negative thinking patterns. If you have tried in vain to get rid of your unhelpful thoughts, don't feel shy to reach out to an authority for help. They understand your problem probably more than you ever will. Get close to people too. You'd be amazed at the number of kind-hearted people out there ready to help you if you choose to want their help.

Chapter 8: How to Change Your Core Beliefs with CBT

Our core beliefs are at the center of the person that we are, i.e., our beliefs about ourselves, others, and life as a whole. Our core beliefs determine how happy we feel about ourselves, our capacity to get along with others, and our potential to achieve the dreams that we hold for our future.

Considering the power that our core beliefs wield, it is critical for every person to have core beliefs that serve to improve their lives, instead of destroying them. Sadly, many people struggle with negative core beliefs, and they ultimately lower the quality of their lives. For instance, if an individual has a core belief along the lines of "I'm foolish", they will shun opportunities that would have led them to great heights and be trapped in a life of mediocrity.

Our core beliefs are the absolute truths and fundamental convictions we have formed about ourselves throughout our lives. To change how you feel, think, and act, you first have to alter your core beliefs. The origins of our core beliefs are varied, but for the most part, they originate from our early childhood. If our dads used to beat on us and call us foolish, we might have internalized the belief that we are stupid. Getting rid of our core beliefs is an extreme challenge, but if we are self-motivated and patient, we can achieve it.

The following are the guidelines for altering our core beliefs:

Deal with One Core Belief at a Time

You can't possibly get rid of all your core beliefs at once. The trick is to deal with one core belief at a time. You want to start with the most powerful core belief. This is the belief that pervades nearly all of your life. Once you identify it, you have to work out a schedule for eliminating this core belief. For instance, if the most dominant core belief of yours is, "I'm a loser", prove yourself that you're no loser. Make a schedule that will guide you in handling various aspects of your life. You want to be in total control.

How Does It Affect Your Life?

Understanding how a certain core belief affects your life will motivate you to change your circumstances. Banking on your introspection, find out how your core belief negatively affects both your personal life and general life. For instance, if you believe that you're ugly, you might not be the most confident person around. Moreover, it can cause you to isolate yourself from other people. In that sense, you lack social support because your core belief holds you back from fitting in with the rest. Understanding the effect that your negative core belief has upon your life is a catalyst for ridding yourself of that negative core belief.

How Much Do You Believe Your Core Belief?

Some of the core beliefs that we hold are utterly ridiculous. Although the conscious mind would view them with suspicion, when it comes to the unconscious mind, it's another story altogether. The unconscious mind gives much weight to our core beliefs. You are supposed to reflect hard and find out how much you believe your core belief to be true. In this exercise, be as honest with yourself as you possibly can, and don't let your ego ruin what you are working on. On a scale of one to ten, rate the extent to which you believe a core belief to be true. Recall various events or experiences that support your level of conviction.

What Is Holding You Back from Changing the Core Belief?

There are three main reasons why we fear changing our core beliefs: fear of failure, fear of uncertainty, and fear of change. If we have kept a certain core belief throughout most of our lives, what will happen if we get rid of it? And more importantly, how will we cope if we fail? To get rid of a negative core belief, you have to be emotionally invested. Becoming conscious of what is holding you back from changing your core beliefs is a great step forward.

Find Ways to Disprove Your Core Belief

Now that you have identified your core belief, and established to what extent you believe in it, the next challenge is to look for evidence that contradicts your core belief. By disproving your core belief, you send a message to your subconscious that this core belief is inaccurate. The subconscious will take notice of the evidence and start altering this core belief. For instance, if one of your core beliefs is, "I cannot make money", go ahead and learn a skill and monetize that skill. When you get money, you're free to point out to your subconscious, "See, I can make money." Eventually, your subconscious will drop that core belief.

Find a New Core Belief

When you are certain that your core belief is fallacious, it's time to get rid of it and create a core belief that captures the truth. For instance, instead of saying, "I hate people," you might say, "I enjoy my own company." That way, negativity is eliminated. Instead of saying, 'I'm a loser," you should say, "I'm quirky."

Explore How Your Life Will Change Thanks to Your New Core Belief

Now that you have acquired a new core belief, explore how it will help you change your life. If you have stopped viewing yourself in a negative light, you might want to think that you are poised to rise to the heights of success – something you never thought possible.

Chapter 9: Benefits of Cognitive Behavioral Therapy in Addiction Treatment

A mind that has been ruined by drug addiction is the perfect breeding ground for negative thoughts and other emotional health issues. Managing challenging thoughts and emotions is hard enough for a sober person, but when you consider a drug addict, the experience is ten times worse. Thankfully, drug addicts can benefit from CBT. Cognitive behavioral therapy has been shown to achieve long-lasting results in the treatment of various addiction types.

The following are some of the benefits of CBT in addiction treatment:

Provides a network of support

Cognitive behavioral therapy allows addicts to have a network of support which is very crucial during the recovery phase. The average addict, if not given positive encouragement, could easily relapse into drug abuse. Therapists are there to offer positive encouragement and gently guide these people toward full healing. When addicts realize that no one cares about them, they are likely to go back to seek solace from drugs. Having a network of support is critical for not only avoiding a relapse but also ensuring general emotional well-being. People are social beings. Thanks to the support network, addicts have someone to talk to.

Increased Positive Thought Patterns

Addicts often struggle with a negative thought pattern that makes them feel helpless; ultimately making them go back to doing drugs. An addict struggles with many bleak thoughts and feelings. However, through the power of positivity, they can overcome their mental and emotional health issues. CBT puts an emphasis on positivity. The more positive an individual is, the less likely they are to slide back into drug addiction. Therapists help addicts overcome their conditions by planting positive thoughts in their subconscious. This helps addicts become positive by default. And whenever they experience emotional troubles, they have someone to guide them.

Enhancement of Self-Esteem

Low self-esteem is one of the reasons why people turn to drug and alcohol. They want to forget their misery and their helplessness. But cognitive behavioral therapy helps addicts develop a great self-image. As their level of self-esteem goes up, they find less desire in escaping reality through drugs and alcohol. They are happy to be themselves. Therapists constantly reinforce addicts' self-esteem and thus raise their desire of wanting a better life than the one they presently have. To get rid of an addiction, the affected person must have the desire of wanting to change their personal circumstances, and this desire becomes natural when an addict's self-esteem is given a boost.

Learning to Resist Peer Pressure

Since we are social beings seeking peer acceptance, it is extremely challenging to resist peer pressure. It is challenging for the average person, and ten times more challenging for the drug addict.

Cognitive behavioral therapy equips addicts with the skills for overcoming peer pressure and focusing on their important life goals. When it comes to resisting peer pressure, they are trained first to imagine saying NO to their peers, and then actually saying NO within a controlled environment. By the end of the training, they won't have any difficulty saying NO to both their peers and anyone else who might be a negative influence.

Cost-Effectiveness

Cognitive behavioral therapy is one of the most affordable addiction treatment methods. Some other treatment methods like rehabs have in-house arrangements for the patient. These treatment methods can be incredibly expensive. Cognitive behavioral therapy can be conducted on an outpatient basis and achieve great results. This treatment method is even covered by insurance plans. Cognitive behavioral therapy is not one-sided. For its success, both the therapist and the patient must work side by side. If the patient is not cooperative, then the treatment will tumble down. Cognitive behavioral therapy is not complicated. It involves general procedures that lead to the restoration of health. There are no expensive or complicated tools required.

Gradual Steps

Overcoming an addiction is no walk in the park. It is a time-consuming quest. Remedies that claim to offer instant results are obviously misleading. In cognitive behavioral therapy, a therapist introduces new principles to the patient as they advance through the treatment. There are principles set aside for the beginners and principles set aside for those who have reached the advanced stage. Walking through these steps, the patient's resolve is strengthened, and they are less likely to run back to drugs or alcohol than patients who have been through any other treatment model. The beauty of cognitive behavioral therapy is that it doesn't advertise itself as a quick fix. It takes real effort to achieve results. However, the effects are long-lasting.

Continuity of Normal Activities

Cognitive behavioral therapy is done on an outpatient arrangement. The patient is free to indulge in other activities for the rest of their time. This is unlike rehabs where patients are held in a campus, effectively suspending their daily engagements such as going to work. With cognitive behavioral therapy, a patient is neither separated from their family nor do they have to seek leave. Because of its flexibility, more people are willing to take this treatment method. And if the sessions are scheduled at night, then your day will run without even a slight hitch.

Gradual End to Therapy

Cognitive behavioral therapy places the entire focus on the patient. The concepts and exercises may be adjusted in accordance with how the patient is faring. In some forms of addiction therapy, the treatment lasts only for a specific amount of time, and then it is cut off. This kind of arrangement doesn't take care of patients who would take ordinarily long to recover fully. In cognitive behavioral therapy, the first few weeks are typically intensive, but as the patient's condition improves, the therapist finds less need to have intensive sessions and focuses on going at the patient's speed of recovery.

Chapter 10: How to use Mindfulness-Integrated Cognitive Behavior Therapy

Mindfulness-integrated cognitive behavior therapy is essentially a therapy approach that incorporates mindfulness training. Mindfulness-integrated cognitive behavior therapy offers a practical set of techniques that are evidence-based, drawn from mindfulness training and concepts of cognitive behavioral therapy, to address an extensive range of mental and emotional health issues.

Mindfulness involves paying full attention to every moment that we experience within our mind and body. We should feel these moments with an accepting attitude, i.e. non-judgmental and non-reactive. Most of our daily emotional health challenges, such as stress, anxiety, and depression, could be overcome by practicing mindfulness.

When we detach ourselves from the events that are going on around us, when we refuse to give negative meanings to events, we increase our capacity to remain unaffected and thus stay grounded.

Mindfulness has an ancient origin some 2,500 years back, and its two most important principles are equanimity and impermanence.

Equanimity

During the day, we go through many experiences, both at the mental and physical level. However, the way we react to these experiences and sensations makes all the difference. Equanimity is the state of giving neutral reactions to anything that happens. If something pleasant goes down, we don't crave it, and if something unpleasant goes down, we develop no aversion toward the experience. It is the state of being balanced, calm, and composed. Developing an equanimous mind is a critical skill in mindfulness because it empowers you to become non-judgmental and non-reactive no matter the experiences that you go through.

Impermanence

Change is the only constant. This applies in the emotional and mental activities of a person too. Regardless of what you feel at the present moment, understand that that feeling will go away, and in its place, another will take over. Mindfulness training emphasizes the impermanence of all things that we can perceive, and in particular, our mental and emotional experiences. As a witness to the changing nature of our internal experiences, we learn to be not only flexible but also objective. When we take on this mindset of being aware of the impermanence of both our emotional and mental experiences, it becomes easier to detach ourselves from views and habits that cause us stress and unhappiness.

Practicing mindfulness

We can practice mindfulness by just having a high state of awareness of the things happening both around and within us. But to develop strong mindfulness skills, we have to take the sitting meditation. The importance of formal mindfulness is that it helps you get rid of stimulations that would take your focus away and keep you from acquiring a deep inner focus. Meditation allows us to savor our internal experiences with a higher level of awareness, neutrality, and acceptance.

The first thing to do in mindfulness meditation is to shut your eyes. Develop your concentration by focusing your breath, and then intensify the attention that you have over your whole being. This serves to get rid of the noise from your mind as well as prevent intrusive thoughts.

Then you enter the phase in which you perceive your thoughts in their naked element. All kinds of thoughts will arise, but don't get caught up in them. See them for what they are: impermanent mental activities, regardless of their subject matter, and go back to the focus of your attention. When you master this process, you will remain unaffected by the thoughts that you experience.

When you give attention to your body sensations, learn to view it as merely a sensation, regardless of its pleasantness or unpleasantness. Training yourself to remain unaffected by your body sensations will allow you to detach from emotions instead of letting emotions be the cause of your suffering.

MiCBT: Integrating Mindfulness and CBT

MiCBT is a four-step therapy made of mindfulness and the basic principles of cognitive behavioral therapy. The goal of MiCBT is to help people modify their feelings and change their unhelpful behaviors. MiCBT takes on a different approach than CBT in helping people modify both their thoughts and behaviors. While CBT focuses on changing people's feelings by modifying their thoughts, MiCBT helps people learn to take control over processes that induce unhelpful thoughts and beliefs by practicing mindfulness.

The Four Stages of MiCBT

Stage One: Personal Stage

In this stage, you learn the basics of MiCBT. You acquire the mindfulness skills of learning about unhelpful thoughts and emotions and detaching from them. At this stage, you get to heighten your awareness and develop an equanimous mind. This allows you to detach from thoughts and take on the role of the observer – not the sufferer.

Stage Two: Exposure Stage

The first stage is about acquiring the basic skills and learning of the projected outcome. In stage two, this is when you get to develop your confidence in your mindfulness skills. Not only are you unaffected by your thoughts, but you are in a capacity to modify your personality so as to fit your philosophy.

Stage Three: Interpersonal Stage

Now that you have learned how not to let thoughts affect your feelings, the next step is to take this attitude to the world. If you seem like a robot, where is your place in society? How do you interact with other people? During this stage, you get to develop your interpersonal and communication skills that will help you interact with people, especially where emotions fly high.

Stage Four: Empathic Stage

In this stage, you learn ways of being more kind to yourself as well as showing others compassion regardless of you being unaffected by their actions or emotions. This stage is aimed at solidifying your state of confidence and improving your level of connectedness with others.

Program Duration

MiCBT can be completed within a relatively short period of time. The MiCBT program takes about eight to twelve sessions. The MiCBT can be tailored according to the needs and personality of the client. In that sense, the length of the program will be informed by the progress of the patient.

Chapter 11: CBT Techniques to Overcome Procrastination

The great writer, Charles Dickens, once said, "Procrastination is the thief of time, collar him."

Aren't we all guilty of putting away a task that we should have done at that moment? If you're the focused kind of person, you have probably recovered from procrastination. Unfortunately, for most people, procrastination is the quiet thief that steals away their dreams. There are many reasons as to why we procrastinate, but for the most part, fear is in the details. You cannot understand why you need to overcome this habit until you first understand the dangers of procrastinating.

The following are some of the ways that we excuse procrastination:

> o *Avoidance:* avoiding the location/situation where the task takes place.
> o *Distraction:* immersing ourselves in other behaviors to forget about the task.
> o *Trivialization:* convincing ourselves that the intended task is not important.

o *Comparisons:* measure our situations up against worse situations

o *Humor:* creating a joke from our procrastination habit.

o *External blaming:* when external forces cause procrastination.

o *Reframing:* thinking that an early start on a project is damaging.

o *Denial:* thinking that the current task is more important than your actual work.

o *Laziness*: being too lazy.

o *Valorization*: being too complacent.

The following are some of the negative effects of procrastination:

- *You lose precious time:* if you tend to procrastinate, at first, it won't seem like you are losing much time. However, understand that this habit will compound, and cumulatively, you will lose a great deal of time. This is the time you should have spent making a positive outcome in your life.

- *You lose opportunities:* they say that an opportunity never knocks twice. Think about all the opportunities you have lost because you never took advantage of them when there was time. Perhaps one of these opportunities might have changed your life for the better, but you blew your chance.

- *You won't be able to meet goals:* this negative habit of procrastination seems to be most potent whenever goals are involved. This might keep you from achieving your important life goals. You may have a strong urge to pursue your goals, but you delay taking the first step for forever, and you end up losing your opportunity.

- *Could ruin your career:* your work ethic has a direct effect on your results. Procrastination may hold you from achieving impressive results, meeting deadlines, and reaching monthly targets. Ultimately, this trend is detrimental to your success.

• *Could lower your self-esteem:* low self-esteem ruins lives in many ways. It causes us to think little of ourselves and believe that we have no power. This negative thought-cycle leads you into even more procrastination. Procrastination not only encourages low self-esteem but actually worsens it. Procrastination not only hinders you from getting started but also poisons your mind into believing that you are inferior.

• *Encourages poor decision making:* when you procrastinate, you tend to make decisions from the wrong footing. This encourages self-deceit. Staying true to yourself is critical while making a decision, but procrastination stops you from making decisions that are objective. Ultimately, you end up becoming a victim of your own poor decisions.

• *You damage your reputation:* procrastination causes you to fail to deliver on your promises. Eventually, people will label you unreliable, and move on to others who can keep their word. People will get warned against working with you. Additionally, procrastination will damage both your self-esteem and self-confidence.

The disadvantages of procrastination are virtually inexhaustible. Luckily, there's a way to overcome procrastination.

The following are some of the CBT techniques that are useful in overcoming procrastination:

Mindfulness

Mindfulness is the process of channeling all your focus into the present moment. There is too much noise – both in our minds and in the physical world. This noise can prevent us from savoring our experiences at a deeper level. However, through mindfulness, we are in a position to give the present time our maximum concentration.

When we give our full attention to the things that we are currently involved in, we are less likely to procrastinate. We can combine mindfulness with CBT to achieve MiCBT. MiCBT aims to equip us with coping skills instead of merely altering our thought patterns. For instance, instead of avoiding conditions that encourage us to procrastinate, we should face those conditions; eventually, we will learn to overcome our procrastination.

Behavioral Activation

This technique aims to help the affected person take on activities that bring them joy. Perhaps their reason for procrastinating is embarking on activities that they don't relish. So getting them to focus on things that they will love is a great step toward helping them step out of their procrastination. For instance, if you want to lose weight, but you tend to procrastinate every time you want to get started on this journey, you might want to find out the weight loss mechanisms that you enjoy, and procrastination won't be an issue anymore.

Behavioral Experiments

Therapists will use behavioral experiments to examine a person's suitability to achieve certain goals. The end goal is to find out the level of optimism or pessimism that a procrastinator carries. Someone might overestimate their ability to achieve so much within a short time – thus procrastinating. In the same breath, someone might be totally pessimistic, so much so that they see no reason to exert any effort. Patients will use various behavioral aspects to stimulate themselves to enjoy various activities and achieve high proficiency. This significantly reduces procrastination.

Voice Training

If you tend to procrastinate because of your vicious inner critic, you could overcome procrastination through voice training. The following are the five steps of voice training:

    o Awareness

o Interrogation
o Analysis
o Fighting
o Maintenance

Chapter 12: Identify Your Important Psychological Needs

The difference between a motivated person and a disinterested person lies in something deceptively simple: the fulfillment of their emotional and psychological needs. Everyone has a set of psychological and emotional needs that they must satisfy in order to feel happy. When a person's important needs are not met, they tend to become frustrated, lose interest, and get depressed. The following are some of the important psychological needs that every person ought to satisfy.

Security

Beneath our rational minds, we are still animals, guided by our animalistic instincts. One of the things that are critical to us is a secure living space. When we have an environment in which we feel safe and taken care of, we can devote our minds to other things. However, if we live in constant fear, we are surely not going to cooperate with ourselves, let alone with anyone else. We are wired to want to take self-preserving actions and seek a secure place for both ourselves and our offspring. Lack of security can give way to various mental and emotional health problems, and in extreme cases, it can lead to loss of mind.

Volition

Every person wants to think that they are one hundred percent in control of their lives. Whether this is possible or not is a subject for debate. If you feel that your sense of freedom is lost or has been threatened, you can have difficulties functioning in a normal society. Having a sense of free will makes a person proud of their achievements because they reckon that they are one hundred percent responsible for their success. Humans will always gravitate toward activities that increase their liberties and people that restrict them less. It's a psychological need that's present in most of us.

Attention

Someone will be quick to say that they don't need anyone's attention. While it may be true that some people don't need the attention of other people, ultimately, everyone needs the attention of the important people in their lives. For instance, if you consider your spouse important, you will crave their attention. Similarly, if you consider your kids important, you will crave their attention. But just the same way that you crave attention, you should be in a position to return the favor. You should lavish your attention on people that consider you important, such as your kids and spouse.

Emotional Connection

Every person craves an emotional connection with another person. We are social beings, and we thrive on being collaborative and helping one another. We certainly require friendship, love, and intimacy. Our emotions are pretty powerful, and we rely on them to navigate through life. If we lack meaningful emotional connections with fellow human beings, it can cause us tremendous pain. Additionally, it can cause other human beings to become wary of us.

A Sense of Status

It is not enough to be part of a group. Additionally, we must prove to ourselves that we add some value to the group. This is what gives us status. We want people to come up to us with their worries, and we will sit them down and ease their pain. Having a status among your peers is a struggle considering that many others want the same for themselves too. However, many perks come with attaining a high status amongst your peers.

A Sense of Achievement

Nothing throws a person into depression and anxiety faster than falling short of their goals. For a person to feel complete, they need to achieve something that they can boast as their own. Whether they are in formal employment or are self-employed, every person has their own long-term goals that they would love to fulfill. If they achieve this goal, they will feel tremendously happy with themselves, but if they fail to achieve their goal, they might become burdened with shame and an immense sense of loss. Becoming an achiever is one way of increasing your status over a wide region.

Meaning

Apart from having a tribe that gives you a sense of belonging and being fulfilled in your own right, you also need to feel as though you're part of something bigger than yourself. It is incredibly important for a human being to have meaning. They will normally align themselves with the philosophies of their higher meaning in life. This way of life causes them to experience joy. Again, having meaning helps one unite with many other people and form a bigger family. Human beings are huge on nesting and creating a sense of belonging. A man whose life has no meaning is fraught with negative thoughts.

Optimism

By default, life is tough. Throughout the world, people are battling challenges. It doesn't matter what position a person holds, but they have challenges that need to be overcome. Thus, a person has to have some sense of optimism. This is the idea that things will get better as time moves on.

Privacy

For our mind and emotional well-being, we require privacy. Privacy goes a long way in preserving our modesty. Without it, we would feel lost and vulnerable. There's the privacy we expect from the big agencies and the privacy we expect from our loyalists.

Validation

Just as we seek the attention of the people we consider important to us, we also seek their validation. We want them to assure us that we are worthy and are doing all right. Lack of validation may sometimes lead to a terrible outcome. For instance, a kid who was never validated by their father might end up seeking validation from the external world by engaging in the controversial behavior, which could ultimately lead them down the path of destruction.

The above are the emotional needs of every person, but still, there are other emotional needs that are person-specific. It is upon you to unravel your psychological needs. Your happiness, to a large extent, depends on the satisfaction of your emotional needs.

Chapter 13: Overcoming Obsessions

It's perfectly normal to check that your door is locked shut occasionally. However, if you suffer from an obsessive personality, you will tirelessly keep checking to see that the door is really shut. Obsessive thoughts and compulsive actions tend to overwhelm a person to the point that they alter normal living patterns. The person becomes helpless against these thoughts.

Obsessive-Compulsive Disorder (OCD) is characterized by uncontainable thoughts and ritualized, recurring behaviors that you are forced to perform. A sufferer of OCD considers their thoughts and behaviors irrational, but still, they are not in a position to resist these repetitive patterns.

The following are the categories of the sufferers of OCD:

- *Washers:* they are afraid of contaminating germs. They have a cleaning compulsion.
- *Checkers:* they recurrently check upon things related to danger or harm.

- *Doubters and sinners:* they are afraid that if everything isn't carried out in a perfect manner, then something terrible will go down.

- *Counters and arrangers:* they have obsessions centered on order and symmetry.

- *Hoarders:* they are scared of throwing anything in their possession away for fear of something terrible happening.

No matter how compulsive the symptoms of your disorder appear, there are numerous techniques of overcoming your condition. The first step is to get rid of the behaviors that arouse your obsessions.

Don't Shun Your Fears

It might seem like a smart move shunning your fears, but the more you run away from your fears, the more you will boost the recurrence of your obsessive patterns and deepen your fears. If you want to get rid of your triggers, learn to endure them for as long as you possibly can. Expose yourself to your OCD triggers and then suppress your urge to perform a ritual. This can be quite challenging if you're not mentally prepared, but you can adjust the intensity of your ritual. The more you expose yourself to your OCD triggers, the lesser your anxiety will become, and ultimately, you will be in a position to take control of your thoughts.

Anticipate OCD Urges

Become aware of situations that trigger your OCD, and take care of them. For instance, if you have an obsession with checking whether the doors are locked, the next time you are locking the door, don't do it just casually and walk away. Carefully lock the door and check to see that it is indeed locked. Don't be in a hurry. When you walk off, you are less likely to battle a compulsion to check the door because you know too well that you ascertained that the door was locked. With your power of imagination, create a vivid image in your mind, depicting the locked door or the shut drapes, and label the image, "The door is locked". Every time you acquire a compulsion to check up on the door or the drapes, you can simply flash the image through your mind, and rightly tag that thought as merely "an obsessive thought".

Refocus Your Attention

Every time you experience an OCD compulsion, don't dwell on it but focus on something else instead. You could work out, go for a jog, read a book, watch a movie, catch up with a friend or listen to music. The idea is to eliminate your OCD compulsion by introducing a new line of thought. When you refocus your attention for at least fifteen minutes, you effectively delay your response to the compulsive thought. When you're done refocusing your thoughts to something else, check up on the original thought, and you will find that the urge will either be feeble or entirely absent.

Write Down Your Compulsive Thoughts

Every person experiences troubling thoughts from time to time. However, people with obsessive-compulsive disorder are stuck in a vortex of compulsion-inducing thoughts. These thoughts keep playing through their mind over and again, up until they indulge in the ritual. You should write down these thoughts as they happen. Using your pen and paper or your favorite gadget, write down any obsessive thought that passes through your mind.

Create an OCD Worry Time

Instead of fighting away your compulsions and thoughts, just reschedule them. During the day, you can have two sessions dedicated to worrying. But you want to have these sessions at a time when you're not vulnerable to anxiety. When you experience compulsive thoughts when it's not worrying-time yet, just write the thoughts down, so that you can think about them during the worrying session.

Create a Recording of Your OCD Obsessions

Record your obsessive thoughts. Focus on a specific obsession and tap it into your gadget. Ensure that you capture their nature extremely well. Then watch or listen over and over to yourself explaining these obsessive thoughts. When you continuously confront your worries and obsessions, you become less affected by them.

Avoid Alcohol and Nicotine

Though alcohol reduces anxiety and worry, the effects last for only a short moment. As the alcohol wears off your system, anxiety becomes much more pronounced. Cigarettes also tend to increase anxiety. When you indulge in these vices, you will be throwing yourself into a bottomless pit of negative thought cycles. You had better face your OCD disorder with a sober mind.

Hang Out with Your Friends and Family More

Obsessive thoughts can plague your life to the point of isolation. But don't let this happen. When you are isolated, the effects of OCD disorder get full blown. Focus on spending time with your loved ones to be more grounded.

Join a Support Group

One of the advantages of living in the modern era is the fact that people who share a common problem are empowered to come together so that they might help one another. Support groups are critical because through sharing and learning from others, you become more empowered to overcome your obsessive compulsions.

Chapter 14: How to Overcome Worry, Fear, Anxiety, and Depression with CBT

At the root of all mental disorders is one critical element known as fear. When it seizes your mind and body, you can only take one direction: down.

Fear is what will cause you to be scared of talking in front of an audience, what will hold you back from asking a member of the opposite sex out on a date, and what will make you shocked when you take an exam. But let's be clear. Fear is not wholly bad. Actually, it's a survival weapon that conditions us to perceive threats within our vicinity and react by either fighting back or escaping.

Anxiety is a type of fear that is tied to the thought of a threat or something terrible happening in the future as opposed to now. A person with an anxiety disorder battles intrusive and obsessive thoughts, as they try to make sense of both their emotions and thoughts.

What Makes You Afraid?

There are very many things that drive us into fear. The origins of our fear are, for the most part, rooted in our childhood experiences. If our guardians instill a fear of darkness in our childhood, we will grow into adults who still fear darkness until the moment we challenge that irrational fear. The first step toward overcoming fear is becoming aware of what you're afraid of and why.

What Makes You Anxious?

Anxiety is merely persistent fear, and it extends to your future. Having an anxiety disorder will surely harm your quality of life. You get into the mindset of seeing problems where there are none. Anxiety puts a quality of extremity to your life so that you're either withdrawn and isolated, or aggressive. Both extremes tend to stifle social cohesion.

How Does Fear Manifest?

When you are frightened or anxious, both your body and mind operate too quick. The following are some of the things that may happen thanks to fear and anxiety:

- Increased heartbeat
- Increased rate of breathing
- Weak muscles
- Profuse sweating
- Stomach pains
- Lack of concentration
- Lightheadedness
- A feeling of getting frozen
- Loss of appetite
- Hot and cold sweats
- Tense muscles
- Dry mouth

The physical symptoms of fear can be very frustrating, especially if you have no idea about the cause of your fear or anxiety. There are various triggers for fear and, sometimes, the brain keeps sending these messages even unnecessarily. You can only improve your capacity to understand your relationship with fear by raising your self-awareness.

Panic Attacks

This is the condition of being overwhelmed by the mental and physical feelings of fear. Sufferers of heart attacks report difficulty breathing, increased heartbeat, and a crazy sensation of losing it.

Worry

This is the magnification of issues so that a person tends to believe that the future is bleak. A worrying individual has a loss of hope, and they expect terrible things to happen at a later time.

The following are some of the techniques for getting rid of your fear, worry, anxiety, depression, and pretty much any other mental disorder:

Face Your Fears

It might sound counterintuitive, but it is the way to go. You gain more power by exposing yourself to your fears rather than running away from them. When you expose yourself to your fears, you gain something valuable: knowledge. Thus, you banish ignorance and realize effective ways of overcoming your anxiety.

Know Yourself

To deliver yourself wholesomely from your fears, you have to spend some time understanding the person that you really are. What are the origins of your fears? What was your childhood like? Knowing that most of our attitudes and fears were formed from early childhood, as well as our experiences, it will be incredibly important to unravel as much as you can about yourself.

Exercise

Performing a workout will require your full attention. Thus, your mind is taken away from its fears and focuses upon the task at hand. This is a great technique of getting rid of your fears and anxiety. Additionally, exercises improve heart health, leading to great blood circulation, a strong immunity, and effectively decreasing bad emotions.

Relax

When you make your body and mind relax, the negative fears will be pushed away. This state of relaxation may be achieved through deep breathing. This involves assuming a meditation position and breathing in and out while clearing the noise from your mind. It helps in restoring the body to a state of balance.

Healthy Eating

Having a clean diet is critical in ensuring that you stay in perfect mental and emotional health. A clean diet focuses on the key nutrients and eliminates junk. You want to keep a healthy blood sugar level. When your blood sugar goes down, you are susceptible to panic attacks and anxiety.

Drink Alcohol in Moderation or Avoid It Altogether

If you are nervous, it can be tempting to down a few bottles. However, understand that the ensuing state of bliss is short-lived. You cannot drink your way into calmness. Instead, learn to face your fears and anxieties while sober. This is more fruitful.

Faith

If you believe in a supernatural entity that oversees the universe and the peoples in it, then it is helpful to trust upon them for deliverance. The more faith you have that this supernatural entity will reach out to you, the better your chances of actually getting rid of your fears and anxieties.

Medication

Medications appeal to people who have time constraints. They may not be the best treatment model, but when combined with other models, the use of medication becomes incredibly helpful.

Support Groups

There are many people battling fears and anxieties just like you. Thanks to the internet, you don't even have to stress out finding these people. They have forums, Facebook groups, websites, and so on. However, before you request to join a support group, make a point of understanding their principles, so that you can weigh up whether you would fit in.

Chapter 15: Methods of Building Solid Self-Esteem

Low self-esteem can be a major hindrance regarding attaining important life goals. The following tips should help you go from low self-esteem to solid self-esteem:

List Your Accomplishments

If you are struggling with feelings of being unworthy, it is easy to lose sight of what you already have. Instead of drowning in a pool of self-pity, you should instead list your accomplishments. These are the things that you are proud to have achieved. Some of these things include your relationships, work, and even home. You don't necessarily have to have a million dollars in your bank account to feel like you have achieved something. All that matters is having a positive attitude. When you list down your achievement, you will realize that you have actually accomplished many things.

Highlight Your Strengths

Perhaps you have lost your confidence due to having negative self-perception and thinking lowly of yourself. The truth is that everyone has their strong points. You just have to look hard enough. Find out what your strengths are and capitalize on them. Your strengths could be along the lines of the following qualities:

o Honesty
o Courage
o Friendliness
o Loyalty
o Self-discipline

Getting to look at the positive things about yourself will surely lift your self-esteem. You will start to look at yourself through the lens of positivity as opposed to negativity. Knowing your strengths and capitalizing on them is the key to success.

Set Goals

Low self-esteem may be brought about by a lack of direction in life. To remedy this, set goals for both the long term and short term, and it will surely increase both your determination and self-confidence. When you have an important life goal to achieve, you are forced to stand up for what you believe in, and in the process, your self-confidence receives a major boost. Self-confidence is not a spiritual thing that you can be bestowed; it is a quality of being that develops within you when you choose to step out of your comfort zone and challenge yourself.

Develop your Assertiveness

Being assertive is the ability to express your needs and wishes, respectfully, and yet respecting the needs and wishes of other people. Perhaps your lack of assertiveness has contributed to your low self-esteem. You develop assertiveness by being conscious of your needs and choosing to stand for what you believe in. Start practicing your assertiveness with the common people in your life. For instance, next time you go into a convenience store, and they get a tiny detail of your order wrong, don't ignore it. Ask them politely to get your order right. If you see someone that you want to talk to, don't hold yourself back. Walk up to them and express yourself. Developing your assertive skills is like growing muscle, the more you challenge yourself, the better you become.

Start Reading Books

When you read voraciously, you kick out ignorance and build up your self-esteem. In this age of the internet, it has even become easy to acquire reading materials. If you become an authority on a certain domain, you will attract people who will want to learn from you, and this will naturally boost your self-confidence. An obvious cause of low self-esteem is ignorance. When you are ignorant about something, you're likely to react in an uneducated way, and this guarantees a blow to your self-esteem. Read extensively – not just the books that will help you develop a certain expertise.

Seek Out Confident Friends

It is true that we become the average of the people we spend most of our time with. If we spend time with losers who are low on self-esteem, it follows that we will become just like them. On the other hand, if we associate with confident people, we get to learn from them, and most importantly, we get to mirror their image. Seeing that self-esteem takes practice, it is essential to have confident friends because they will help you "talk the language of high self-esteem". For instance, your friends will help you give appropriate responses to many situations that you find yourself in.

Help Others

This is another secret of raising your self-esteem. Helping others first of all makes you feel good about yourself. Being altruistic will also make you feel good about yourself, but more importantly, it will trigger a sense of self-worth in you. The more you view yourself in a great light, the more you increase your self-esteem. Helping others is also a way of expanding your network – unless we are talking about someone who cannot do anything at all. When you help someone, they will go on to do amazing things with their lives, and they will become an asset for you, not a liability.

Expand your Social Circle

Developing great social skills is critical in boosting your self-esteem. At the end of the day, we are social beings who rely on social proof and need the input of others to fulfill our important physical and psychological needs. The more adept you are at communicating with others, the more you strengthen your self-esteem. However, you have to be careful in the selection of the people you hang out with. Don't hang out with bad elements of society.

Challenge Yourself

Another way of developing self-esteem is through challenging oneself. Most people want to stay in the comfort zone. But there's no progress made in the comfort zone. However, if you take up a challenge, you will make yourself raise your standards and learn a thing about character. In this way, you will boost your self-esteem.

Do the Things that you are Good At

At the end of the day, we are all gifted differently. To achieve true happiness, we have to do something that we enjoy. We are also likely to have more confidence in ourselves when we take up challenges and activities that we enjoy doing.

Chapter 16: How to Overcome Anger and Bitterness Using CBT

At one point, each one of us has gotten so angry we couldn't think straight. Anger and bitterness are very potent feelings. They can influence us in a major way.

Yet, anger is not entirely bad. This feeling helps us alert the world to our needs and the fact that people are not responding to them. Anger can stir you into taking swift action.

But then there's the dark side to anger. Sometimes, we may get irritated for no reason at all. Other times, we may get angry with people for the flimsiest of reasons. The media is full of examples of people who are too angry and are venting out at the world by committing awful crimes.

This is the point you have to draw a line and start reclaiming yourself back. You don't want your anger to lower the quality of your life by antagonizing everyone and ending up on your own or making people pay dearly for associating with you.

What Leads to Excessive Anger?

Our anger stems from very diverse areas. However, for the most part, we tend to drag our anger from our past, and more specifically, our childhood. If we had sadistic parents who hurt us and made us feel terrible, we might end up becoming angry, bitter adults.

The following are some of the major factors that lead to excessive anger:

Believing That We Have Been Mistreated

A human being's sense of self-preservation is much heightened. People are very sensitive to scenarios that are aimed at inflicting pain into their lives. This is because our brains are designed to eliminate the bad experiences, the discomfort, and only seek the things that will make us happy. If a boss mistreated you, it could lead to anger, and depending on the extent of mistreatment, it can worsen into bitterness, so that you resent your boss to the point of wishing them the worst, and hoping to get a chance to exact your vengeance.

Selective Attention

For some crazy reason, we tend to find supporting evidence for the things that bother us, i.e., if you're focused on the negative side, then it becomes more pronounced; thus triggering your anger. For instance, if you believe your spouse is not on the same page as you, you will tend to notice the things that about them that aggravate you or the times that they lambast you, and ignore all their good deeds. If you are concerned about road rage, you will only notice the bad-mannered drivers, and ignore the good drivers. Such a mindset can spark immense anger and bitterness.

Biased Thinking

In a way, biased thinking is tied to an inability to perceive things objectively. If you're not objective, you will always think that people have a hidden agenda of disappointing you or making you feel bad. You will think that people are deliberately inconsiderate of your needs. When you have a biased mindset, you experience more anger and bitterness than other people. For instance, if you hold some inaccurate beliefs about a minority group, the day that a person will serve you from that minority group, it doesn't matter their qualifications, you are still more inclined toward being angered by their actions.

If you are stuck in this negative cycle of needlessly experiencing anger, don't despair. With enough dedication, you can overcome this challenge.

The following are some of the critical CBT techniques that will help you get rid of your anger and bitterness:

Monitor Your Thoughts

Whenever you realize that you are experiencing anger or bitterness, try to explore the contents of your mind. Are there feedback loops that have misled you? Find out if you have an error in judgment. And also, find out if there's an alternative way of perceiving the situation to make it more accurate and lessen the irritation. Always stay aware of your thoughts.

Know Your Triggers

Some scenarios or people are more likely to make us angry or bitter than other scenarios or people. This is what we call triggers. For instance, discussing money matters with your spouse can be a trigger for your anger, and so is meeting a person that you hold a grudge against. If you are aware of your triggers, you can either avoid them or prepare yourself mentally to stay grounded.

Get Rid Of Your Entitlement

Your entitlement usually flashes with the thoughts of "should". Like, "They should treat me better," or "They should accept what I'm saying." The more entitled you are, the less happy you will be. This is because you will encounter people who absolutely don't care about your feelings. Learn to tame your "should" thoughts.

Get Enough Sleep

We are less likely to tolerate irritating behaviors when we are short on sleep. And then again, we tend to be impulsive when are sleep deprived. For instance, something that we'd have normally been unbothered with will cause us to lash out in anger due to lack of sleep. Knowing this, you should always ensure that you get enough quality sleep.

Give Yourself Enough Time

We are more likely to become angry when there's a sense of urgency, and we are running out of time. This is why newsroom editors are proverbially terse to be around. Give yourself enough time to process things, and you will adjust appropriately. When your brain finds out that you are in control, it becomes less inclined to switch the alarms on.

Assert Your Needs

Don't let the negative experiences compound. Learn to assert your needs as soon as the occasion presents itself. For instance, if your spouse does something that irritates you, then say it at the time that they have done it. Otherwise, those irritations will slowly build up inside of you, and at the breaking point, you will explode at your spouse, saying things you would never have said if you had been grounded.

Chapter 17: Make Peace with Your Past

The famous psychologist, Carl Jung, once said, 'I'm not what happened to me. I am what I choose to become."

Time flies by, and no matter what, life moves on. Our past holds all sorts of things: wins, losses, and even pain. We forget about most of the things that happened to us and move on. However, there are specific events that happened in our past that still hold us prisoner. We have refused – or are incapable – of letting go of these past traumas, and as a result, they affect our present lives.

These past traumas have become the fuel behind our mental and emotional health issues. Before you learn about ways of making peace with your past, you first need to understand why you should stop living in the past.

> • *You cannot change the past:* there are no rehearsals to life. Whatever happened, you cannot go back to modify it. So, you have two options: to be held a prisoner of that event or to look into your future with a fresh perspective.

- *Challenges make you a stronger person:* think about it, there are billions of human beings on this planet. It would take something out of the norm to stand out amongst all these people. Overcoming your past challenges is a surefire way of standing out as a strong person and a role model. If you think along this line, you will be more enthusiastic about making peace with your past.
- *It is incredibly freeing:* making peace with your past means that you're ready to let go of the baggage that you have always carried around. When you let go of this baggage, you will truly become free, which will do wonders for your mental health.

Making peace with your past is not as easy as it may sound. Remember that you're making the conscious decision to remain unaffected by significant events that took place in your past.

The following are helpful points to get you started on the journey of making peace with your past:

Recognize That It's Time to Move On

You have been held a prisoner of your past for far too long. Making the conscious decision of letting go of your past is going to hurt your ego, as though you have admitted defeat, but it is the right thing altogether. It shows that you have insight and are willing to change your situation.

Make a List of the Lessons That Your Past Taught You

There are no rehearsals to life. It's happening. However, you should also realize that what goes around comes around. You can't close off the possibility that something of a similar nature to an event from your past is going to repeat itself. For instance, if your past was marked with irresponsible sexual behavior that left you a young parent or drug abuse that cost you your loved one, make a list of the lessons that you learned from these traumatic events. Probably events of a similar nature are going to show up in your future, but knowing what you know, you will be better placed to make the right decision.

Believe in Yourself

You can overcome any challenge. But to achieve that, you first need to cultivate a strong sense of self-belief. And self-belief is nothing more than realizing that you're up to the task. You will have to drop the victim mentality and begin the necessary work to turn your life around.

Meditate

We live in a noisy and chaotic world – add to that the fact that you are carrying baggage from your past, and then you have one stewing bomb of emotional troubles. Thankfully, you can calm your mind and clean your emotions through meditation. All you have got to do is find a serene environment, assume the formal meditation stance, and take long, deep breaths with focused intention.

Practice mindfulness

When you are a prisoner of your past, there's nothing in your present life that is interesting enough. You could be having a supposedly deep conversation with your friend, but your mind is still ruminating about a past trauma. Being a prisoner of your past hinders you from enjoying your present. What to do? Get into mindfulness. Mindfulness is the practice of focusing your whole attention on what's happening at present. It doesn't matter whether you're eating or talking to a baby; give your present moment your undivided attention.

Get Rid of your Fear

The traumas of your past have most likely instilled some fears in you. Learn to overcome these fears by challenging yourself. For instance, if you once loved deeply, and the object of your love did the dirty on you, that event might have hardened your heart, so that you find it difficult to love another person. Get rid of this fear by actually loving again. Your attitude of wanting to make progress will eventually bear fruit. When you rid yourself of your fears, you will also have clarity of thought, which is a critical ingredient for success.

Forgive

Someone did you wrong, and you have never gotten over it. This becomes your thirst for an opportunity to exact your vengeance. If this is you, you're doing a great disservice to yourself. The energy you allocate toward sustaining your grudges could be better spent in achieving your goals. Learn to forgive. Make peace with whoever hurt you in your past. This deed is incredibly freeing.

Count Your Blessings

This deceptively simple technique can force you to take a whole new perspective on your life. In the grand scheme of things, your problems are really pointless. If you take a moment to list the things that you are grateful for, you will realize that you're indeed blessed, and have no reason to pine. However, if you're an ungrateful person, there are not enough blessings in the world to satisfy you, and it would be akin to trying to fill up a bottomless pit.

Chapter 18: Secrets of Developing the Best Attitude

Many studies have found that your attitude makes the difference between achieving success and becoming a failure. You might be a very qualified individual, but if your attitude is nasty, you will end up achieving less than an underqualified person with a great attitude. In many fields of work, success is down to the collaborative skills of individuals, and if you have a poor attitude, you will make a poor teammate.

A negative attitude is a psychological impediment to success, but even worse, it makes people shun you. If you have a terrible attitude, you are going to have a terrible time of it. Thankfully, your poor attitude is not set in stone. You can change it if you choose to.

The following are some of the secrets of developing a warm attitude that will draw people in and also open you up to opportunities:

Stop Acting Entitled

When you act entitled, you send the message that you have too high an opinion of yourself. This will antagonize other people, and you will have zero allies. When you are on good terms with people, you have the best environment for cultivating a great attitude.

Be Grateful

If someone shows you kindness, the least you can do is appreciate their effort. People notice those who never appreciate their kind gestures. It reeks of entitlement. Be grateful in small and big things alike. It will help you establish connections and enter into mutually beneficial relationships.

Improve Your Lifestyle

Your lifestyle has a great influence on the person you end up becoming. If you're into binge drinking and spending your weekends laughing around with female or male hookers, it would be quite challenging to develop a great attitude. A great attitude goes together with a certain awareness of a moral compass. So, cut out the drunken weekends, and channel that time into spending time with your loved ones. Another important aspect of your lifestyle is your diet. Cut out the junk and start preparing healthy meals. Healthy meals are not only good for your emotional and mental health but also your wallet.

Reframe Your Challenges

Regardless of the challenges that you might be facing, never assume a rigid approach. Look at your challenges from various angles. The more flexible you are, the more creativity you stir in yourself, and ultimately, you will be in a far better position to solve your challenges.

Embrace Rejection

Harden your heart a little bit so that rejection won't cripple you. The fact of the matter is that on the path to reaching your goals, you are going to get rejected more times than you will care to remember. Read about movie stars and the rejection that they go through. When you learn to embrace rejection, you elevate yourself into the mindset of an unstoppable winner.

Use Positive Words

If you have a negative attitude, it follows that negative words will escape your mouth when describing your life. You will always come from a perspective of lack and misery. Change this pattern by starting to say positive things about yourself. Look at your glass as half full – not half empty.

Become a Doer

Instead of talking about the grand plans that you haven't acted upon yet, make a rule of talking about the things you have actually done. This will push you into becoming more of a doer than merely a talker. For instance, instead of saying, "I'll drop my CV to twenty offices this week," it should be, "This week, I dropped my CV to twenty offices."

Become Wary of Energy Vampires

Sadly, not everyone in your life is well-meaning. Various people act like a vampire – they drain your energy. When you discover an energy vampire, you want to pull away from them as quickly as you can, so that they don't deplete your positive energy.

Deep Breathing Exercise

There is a direct relationship between our breathing and our emotions. When we are constricted and have trouble breathing, we become susceptible to negativity. However, when we inhale oxygen-rich air on the regular, we tend to become grounded. Practice deep-breathing exercises and watch your negative thinking patterns fade away.

Choose to See the Positive Side

No matter how bleak the situation appears, always choose to see the brighter side of things. If your company posts losses, don't wallow in despair but choose to see it as an opportunity to prove your mettle. If your company posts massive profits next year, you will reclaim your top spot, and inspire others. Always choose to see the bright side of things.

Be More of a Problem-Solver

A negative person points out problems for the sake of tearing things down. They rejoice in bringing people down to their level. But you should place as much thought into the solution as you place into the problem. Instead of criticizing and leaving it at that, offer a solution, and the other party will appreciate your criticism.

Become the Agent of Joy

There is no shortage of sadists in the world. However, there aren't enough people to spread joy, which is what we need more of. Become the agent of spreading joy around the world. When you have a positive impact on the lives of people, it increases your self-esteem and challenges your natural selfish tendencies.

Cultivate Meaningful Relationships

When you're in a relationship, you learn to become a giver, not always a taker. Being selfless is a vital element of a positive attitude. As a giver, you operate from the mindset of abundance, and this leads you to become a resourceful person.

Develop Crisis Management Skills

Whatever happens is not the actual problem, but your reaction is where the problem is. You cannot escape crises for as long as you are alive. However, if you have crisis management skills, you are far more likely to emerge out of the situation unscathed, and yet preserve your good image.

Chapter 19: Critical Lifestyle Changes

Your lifestyle forms the person that you are. If you want to experience change, you first may have to modify your lifestyle.

The following are great tips to help you improve your lifestyle:

Travel

There's a whole lot of truth to the maxim, "Traveling broadens the mind." The more traveled you are, the greater your insight into human life. Traveling doesn't have to be expensive. Whether you would like to travel in a far away country or just in America, there are many professional bodies to help you save money and help you have the best experience.

Change your Job

The simple truth is that a majority of people are trapped in jobs that are slowly, irreversibly, sucking the soul out of them. However, most of these people are scared of leaving their jobs because they don't know what waits in the future. They ask themselves questions such as: "What if I fail to get another job?" Or, "What if I become a failure?" But if you have had enough with a terrible job, you want to risk it all, knowing too well that this is your chance to become truly free.

Move House

If you have lived in one place for decades, you might want to change that. Moving houses allows you to experience a new culture and even new friends. This may necessitate the selling of your house, but it's still fine. Humans share a great capacity to connect with each other, and no matter where you go, you will always find a tribe that will accept you.

Become a Volunteer

When you're a volunteer, you are in a position of blessing others with your most important resource – time. The appreciation you receive also humbles you. However, more importantly, serving as a volunteer gives you an opportunity to see that you're indeed blessed. Some people depend on others for the satisfaction of their emotional and physical needs. If you weigh your troubles against theirs', you will recognize that you're blessed, lucky even.

Break the Routine

Maybe you have settled into a routine, and you have reduced yourself into a kind of robot. Every single thing that you do is informed by a routine. Guess what? Break all the rules! Start by taking different routes to work, changing what you eat, and visiting places that you are not accustomed to.

Set a Goal

Instead of letting your life waste away like a blind loser, you should set a goal. If you have set a goal, you will increase both your self-esteem and zeal for living. Your goals don't necessarily have to be focused on changing the world. It is enough just to want to save up for a new car.

Do Something That Scares You

If you have been living in a safe space for forever, this thought of exposing yourself to danger terrifies you. But think about the benefits of conquering your fears. You will increase your self-esteem and develop a winning attitude. Get into the habit of doing something that scares you periodically.

Challenge Yourself

In other words, get out of your comfort zone. It doesn't matter what you do, but if you put a little more effort into your work, if you go the extra mile, you will always stay ahead of your competition. Getting out of your comfort zone will go a long way in boosting your mental health.

Write Every Day

Scientific studies have proven that writing has a therapeutic effect. If you're feeling overwhelmed, all you have to do is get a pen and some paper or open your computer and start writing away. You can write about your feelings, or you can even write fiction. When you make this a daily habit, you will strengthen your mind.

Become More Active

If your normal day involves waking up, taking a shower, eating breakfast, driving to work, eating fries for lunch, coming back home in the evening to slump in your couch and watch TV as you eat dinner till you fall asleep, then you're doing your body a great disservice. Start getting active by, for example, working out.

Improve Your Looks and Image

Your image can greatly affect how others perceive you. If you are always wearing faded out or wrinkly T-shirts and look shabby, people will hardly respect you, let alone like you. You have to improve your looks so that people start taking you seriously.

Improve your wardrobe and pay more attention to your personal grooming.

Get Quality Sleep

Ensure that every night you get at least six hours of sleep. If you have quality sleep, you will always have the energy to face your day, and you'll be pleasant to be around. However, if you are deprived of sleep, you are likely to be a pain, and you won't meet your obligations with enough dedication.

Improve your Diet

There's a whole lot of truth to the maxim, "You're what you eat." If you are used to a crappy diet, you will both feel and look like crap. The first thing that needs to go is the junk, for its loaded with too much sugar that overwhelms the body and makes us susceptible to degenerative diseases, such as cancer. Then, you need to consume water regularly to ensure that your physiological processes are optimal.

Ditch Bad Influences

The most common source of bad influences is the people and things you give your time to. If you keep friends with dangerous people who do drugs and commit crimes, they are bound to influence you into becoming one of them. You had better resist their attempts to draw you in by being a no-show in their lives. If you keep friends with toxic people and seem unwilling to take on their toxicity, they can resent you and cause you harm.

Watch less TV

TV is not so much an entertainment platform as it is a marketing platform. The producers want to flash ads to as many eyeballs as possible so that they can make massive sales. Staying away from TV is not only great for your wallet, but it also frees up your time to do the things that really matter. For instance, writing.

Chapter 20: Thinking Errors That Deplete Your Mental Energy

Three critical factors contribute to our mental strength:

- o Controlling our emotions
- o Managing our thoughts.
- o Staying productive regardless of the conditions

These three factors are challenging, yet managing your thoughts is the hardest challenge of all. Our thoughts are not always realistic. Sometimes, we endure illogical and impractical thoughts. When we accept our illogical thoughts, we inadvertently distort our capacity to be true to both ourselves and others.

The following are some of the inaccuracies in our thoughts that deplete our mental energies:

All-Or-None Mode of Thinking

Sometimes, we see things as being black or white. We never pause to consider the gray area. If you're looking for an employee, the black or white approach might make you lose out on hiring a great person. In as much as we have a tendency of seeking patterns to every situation, this approach doesn't always work. We should be flexible enough to consider the things that exist in the fringes. Being able to look at a project not merely in the success or failure terms, being willing to explore the hidden dimensions beyond the superficial, calls for a certain level of maturity.

Overgeneralizing

It's quite easy to witness one instance and then draw a blanket judgment. Humans are pattern-seeking beings. We want to unravel the mysteries so bad that we will stop at nothing in our quest. For instance, if we have a run-in with one person, we might look to their background and assume that people of that background wholly have a problem with you. If we had been objective, we would have focused on the one person, but the instinct wouldn't let us. We need to identify threats as quick as humanly possible. For instance, if someone in your class is rude to you, you might think to yourself, *The whole class hates me!*

Filtering Out the Positive

We may achieve a lot but fail to lay emphasis on our achievements, yet we will emphasize the tiny thing that goes wrong. If we closed nine deals, and toward the end of the day we lost a single deal, we may focus on what we lost and become blind to what we already achieved. Filtering out the positive not only discourages us from capturing reality but also acts as a trigger to needless negativity. To have a balanced life, we are supposed to look at both the positive and negative sides of a situation.

Mind-Reading

Some people act as though they were mind-readers of some sort. The simple truth is that it is impossible to know what is going through another person's mind. When we meet a business rival, and they seem uncomfortable, we might say to ourselves, "She is mad at me because my business is doing better than hers," but there are millions of probabilities that she had been thinking something entirely different. If you haven't heard someone lend a voice to their thoughts, never make the mistake of trying to read their minds – because you're most likely to fail anyway.

Catastrophizing

This is the tendency of imagining that things are worse than they actually are. People with anxiety disorders are most susceptible to this thinking error. For instance, if someone that you deeply care about comes down with an illness, you may lose it and start running around thinking that they are going to die. Just because they have fallen sick doesn't mean that they have reached their end. This tendency of catastrophizing events and conditions ultimately creates a negative mindset. Such a person expects only the worst from life, and thanks to their negative attitude, they'll succeed in attracting appalling incidents.

Emotional Reasoning

We are emotional beings, and for the most part, our emotions inform both our beliefs and actions. If we are nursing terrible thoughts, the chances are that we will acquire terrible beliefs as well as act in a terrible manner. Emotional reasoning causes the affected person to trust their emotional thoughts and actualize them. For instance, if you think, *I'm such a loser,* that statement will convince you that you are a loser, and moreover, it will cause you to act like one. But emotional reasoning can be helpful if it is of a positive nature. For instance, when you think, *I'm such a winner*, it will cause you to believe this thought and start acting like one.

Labeling

People are social beings. We like doing things as a group. And we actually increase our chances of attaining success when we work as a team as opposed to being isolated. However, as we mix with others, we are going to witness people behave in ways that we don't approve. Instead of trying to understand them, we might label them with derogatory terms. This tendency of labeling events and behaviors is in line with our primal instinct of unraveling patterns. When we are witness to unpleasant behaviors or events, our first reaction ought not to be labeling, but seeking to understand.

Predicting

This is when we take up the role of fortune tellers. For instance, if we have a presentation the next day, we might say, "I'm going to embarrass myself tomorrow." Since you have planted this negative expectation in your mind, it actually raises your chances of embarrassing yourself. Behaving like a fortune teller and focusing on negativity can easily make your prophecy self-fulfilling.

Taking Things Personally

A person who takes things personally tends to have a victim mentality. They will normally think that the world is against them. If they apply for a job and receive no invitation for a job interview, they will assume that employers are against them. If they try to woo a member of the opposite sex in vain, they will think that all members of the opposite sex hate them.

Chapter 21: CBT as A Treatment for PTSD

If you have lived through or witnessed a shocking, scary or dangerous event, you might develop a condition known as Post-traumatic Stress Disorder. These traumatic events range from losing a house to fire, losing a loved one, or surviving a road accident. The more an event excites horror, helplessness, serious injury or death, the more potent the PTSD.

Main Symptoms of PTSD

> • *Re-experiencing symptoms:* this is where a person relives the terrible experiences in their minds. If the traumatic event they went through had been a loss of their house by a fire that even claimed one of their loved ones, the affected person might start having flashbacks of the event. Traumatic events tend to make a person feel helpless, and when they come back to haunt them in the form of flashbacks or intrusive thoughts, the affected person feels drained of energy. They lose their capacity to move on with the rest of the day after re-experiencing the traumatic event through their mind's eye.

- *Avoidance symptoms:* sufferers of PTSD tend to avoid events or situations that might lead them to think back to their traumatic event. For instance, if someone had lost their loved one through a water accident, whereby their boat capsized, the sufferer may actively avoid ever getting into a boat again. This is because if they entered the boat, they would have no peace at all, a mixture of fearing that whatever happened to their loved one might happen to them, and getting to relive the horrific event in their mind.

- *Hyperarousal symptom:* if you have lived through a traumatic event, it can modify your nervous system in such a way that you become too sensitive. For instance, you could become anxious at the ring of a loud noise, or the flash of a bright light. These are merely your survival instincts kicking into gear. Additionally, you could have trouble falling asleep or getting to concentrate. Such problems would embitter your life, eliminate happiness, and potentially ruin your life too.

- *Cognition and mood symptoms:* another obvious sign of PTSD is an inability to remember the exact details of the traumatic event. The rush of adrenaline you had experienced back then might be responsible for blocking out some of the details. Then you might experience guilt or blame someone for what happened. If you think that you had a chance of mitigating the trauma, but failed to, you will experience an immense amount of guilt. Additionally, PTSD can make you lose interest in activities that you once enjoyed.

There are a number of ways of treating Post-traumatic Stress Disorder, but one of the most effective ways involves the use of CBT. Actually, it is believed to be the most effective form of treatment, with people living with PTSD getting rid of their symptoms in as short as twelve sessions.

The following are some of the methods used in treating PTSD:

Prolonged Exposure

If someone has lived through a traumatic event, it is only natural to want to stay away from the thought patterns that would call back those traumatic memories. However, this treatment method seeks to do just that: expose the person to the memories of the trauma for an extended amount of time. The logic behind this treatment method is that once the person with PTSD confronts their fears, they will eventually stop being bothered. However, if they keep running away, then the traumatic memories will hold a lot of power over the individual. As a subject of numerous scientific studies, this treatment method has received praise for being effective in eliminating re-experiencing symptoms, anxiety arousal, and avoidance of PTSD-arousing stimuli. Positive results can be achieved by the third session.

Cognitive Processing Therapy

When a traumatic event takes place, the affected person might develop various maladaptive assumptions that will increase the potency of their trauma. Cognitive processing therapy is used in detecting and restructuring the maladaptive patterns in their thoughts. This method helps people with PTSD find meaning out of the trauma, and it also helps decrease their anxiety and boost their self-esteem. Cognitive processing therapy has been shown to have a high success rate of curing PTSD symptoms. To a large extent, the success of this treatment model is down to the sufferer, i.e., they must be cooperative.

Seeking Safety

When you live through a traumatic event, your emotional makeup might become twisted. For instance, if you survive a road accident, you will become an extremely sensitive person. Something as ordinary as experiencing a bump while riding a car will suddenly make you fearful, cause a flood of emotions, and it will take a long time to return to normal. Seeking safety helps people to overcome their emotional dysregulation and cope with their extreme fears. One of the ways of curing emotional dysregulation is through practicing mindfulness. When your mind is focused on savoring the present moment, it is less likely to jump back to the traumatic past.

Eye Movement Desensitization Reprocessing

EMDR is much like prolonged exposure, except that it utilizes eye movement exercises. This treatment was popular a few years back but seems to have fallen out of favor with therapists since the evidence came out that the eye movement exercises achieved nothing. However, some therapists still employ this method of treatment. In keeping with the tradition of prolonged exposure, the sufferer is made to relive their trauma, through their minds, and then the therapist guides them in performing various eye exercises.

Chapter 22: Eight Ways to Rewire Your Brain Using CBT

Everyone has gone through a terrible phase during which they endured depression. When depression comes knocking, it seeks to expose you and make you vulnerable, break you, and you are left feeling as though the weight of the world has been placed upon your shoulders. Your brain might be entangled in a vicious fight, but don't reach for the antidepressants. You have a much better chance at rewiring your brain through CBT.

The following are some of the CBT techniques aimed at modifying your brain into positivity:

1. Set achievable goals

Before you get started on your therapy, you want first to identify what you seek to get out of it. The last time you were depressed, you knew too well what could end your depression. Ideally, this ought to be one of your goals. To avoid disappointments, you want to ensure that your goals are reachable. If you set unattainable goals, you will only be setting yourself up for more failure, which might throw you into an even worse state of depression. When setting a goal, you should implore the help of your therapist because they have a finer understanding of the potential that different kinds of people wield, as well as the nature of various challenges.

2. Reward yourself

The perfect way of motivating yourself to keep going is to reward yourself every time you reach a milestone. When you set a long-term goal, you should make a point of breaking it down into smaller milestones. For instance, if the cause of your depression is due to the fact that you have no life partner, your mid-term or long-term goal should be getting a life partner, but your milestones should be along the lines of talking to a new person every day. Ensure that you talk to someone new every day. This increases your prospects of landing the most suitable life partner. Every time you reach this milestone, you might want to reward yourself for work well done.

3. Be good at spotting negativity at its onset

The more adept you are at noticing negativity creep up on you, the more you will take self-preserving decisions. Let's say that your depression is enhanced by your alcoholism, which is in part fueled by your associations. When you see a person who takes you into a bar and buys you a beer, you might want to literally run away from them. Whenever you identify an agent of negativity, you should want to distance yourself from them. However, this doesn't give you a free pass to become a weirdo. In as much as you want to preserve yourself, you also have to consider what's at stake.

4. Be accountable

Being accountable is the truest sign of maturity. Let's say you are depressed because of your gambling behavior. You seem to have been stuck in a negative cycle of throwing your money into sports betting, taking loans from friends and banks, and then throwing more money into sports betting. So, betting has become this big black hole where your every penny drowns. You'll become depressed, and rightly so. But think about it. When you're accountable for something – for instance, your family – you won't spend your money that recklessly. You will have some respect for your family, and other people that hold you responsible.

5. Listen to music

It is an open secret that listening to music has a great effect on our moods. Whenever you find yourself battling depressive thoughts, all you have to do is put on some music. The brain is extremely receptive of music, and it allows you to take on the mood expressed in the music. For instance, if you listen to a happy song, your moods will be instantly elevated. In this age of the internet, there's a surplus of great music to listen to. Remember that striking a balance is vital – don't lose yourself, lest it becomes an addiction, an escape from reality.

6. Join a group

Whatever you are facing now, whatever brings you gloomy thoughts, and depresses your spirit, is not unique to you. There are millions of other people battling the same problems. And guess what? They are every bit as interested in overcoming their limitations just as you. You can contact friends and make phone calls to various offices to find out about groups that cater to people of your kind. Additionally, you can join online groups and become united with people from around the world who share in your troubles. Seeing other people from diverse backgrounds in the same boat as you not only gives you hope for change, but it also allows you to become vulnerable. For instance, if your addictions are the source of your depression, you can share your story with your group members, make it a learning opportunity, and be open to learning from them too.

7. Focus on positive experiences

The most potent fuel for depression is a negative attitude. And if you have a negative mindset, nothing in this world would cure your problem. This is simply because every event or situation is two-sided. There's the good side and the bad. Negative people always choose the bad, whereas positive people choose the good. It doesn't matter if you're ruined financially, if you have lost your career to malicious people, or if you've ever lost a loved one. There's always a positive angle to every situation.

8. Consume the right media

It's amazing that when people talk about the advances in technology and especially digital media, they focus on the negative effects. It's true that most people on the internet are watching pornography, but the internet has also brought close to us amazing content of positivity. There are eBooks, websites, and YouTube channels that cater to promoting positivity. Instead of replenishing your positivity just once and moving on with your life, you want to graduate this into a habit. Form a daily habit of checking up on YouTube positivity channels and reading positivity blogs and eBooks.

Chapter 23: Ten Introductory Questions Therapists Commonly Ask

The success of any therapy largely depends on the efforts of both parties. If an experienced therapist meets up with an uncooperative patient, the results will be less than appealing. So it is critical for both parties to get along. When a therapist first meets their client, they have to ask them questions. These questions are aimed at understanding the client's challenges, past experiences, philosophies, and goals.

The following are some of the questions that a therapist may ask their client during their first meeting:

What brings you here?

This is likely the first question that will escape their mouth. The therapist is interested in knowing why their client chose them. There are many practices – both private and public – that offer CBT programs, but there has to be a reason why this client chose that practice. A client must not be shy of letting a therapist know that, for instance, they did their research and found glowing reviews about the practice. Therapists get flattered when they know that past clients were appreciative of their efforts and that they are making a positive impact.

Have you ever seen another counselor before?

A therapist is interested in knowing if their potential client has seen a counselor or counselors before. They might ask the number of counselors you have met, and even explore the nature of the treatment you received, and whether or not the treatment bore the results you had hoped for. If the results were pleasant, did they last? They might also want to know about the one thing that stood out about your previous counselors. The therapist wants to understand the kind of relationship you had with your previous counselor(s).

From your perspective, what is the problem?

People can have varied viewpoints to just one problem. When a therapist asks this question, they are hoping to shine a light on the quirky traits of their potential client. There's not a single anointed way of approaching a problem. The goal is to effect positive change with the least resources and as quickly as humanly possible. However, to tailor the CBT program to a client's needs and personality, the therapist has to understand the particulars of their potential client's problem. For instance, what role have other people played in their troubles? What is their personality like? What are their accomplishments? Who are the most important people in their lives?

On the whole, how does this problem make you feel?

When a therapist poses this question, they know too well that you are already battling some challenges. But this question is designed to highlight your attitude. They want to know where their potential client lies on the spectrum between optimism and pessimism. The tools for handling a pessimist are wildly different from the tools for handling an optimist. However, they have a genuine interest in knowing their client's true feelings.

What makes the problem better?

The therapist is interested in knowing whether their potential client has had success before in dealing with the problem that bedevils them at present. They want to know how many times the problem recurs within a specific period of time and what factors worsen or improve the problem. The therapist wants to know the resources their client has channeled into curing that problem and what effect the problem has created on their lives. Has it affected their self-esteem? Has it made them guilty? How are the reactions from friends and family?

If you had the powers, what positive changes would you make in your life?

This question is aimed at getting a glimpse of the client's goals. Of course, the client would want to actualize the various things that they have set as goals. The therapist is also interested in hearing about their attitude toward change. With so much power, the power to do anything, a person's attitude is definitely going to change. And then again, it helps the therapist understand their client's threshold for pain. A client who would eliminate all the challenges and difficulties from their life is the kind of person with a low tolerance for pain.

How would you describe your mood on the whole?

People experience different moods at different times. Some people have stable moods, whereas others are always in a roller coaster of moods. And then there are people who hardly ever seem affected. They seem like robots, distant and cold. A therapist is determined to find out what really changes the moods of their clients. What makes them happy or sad? And more importantly, what are their coping strategies? Do they get into alcohol and sex as a way of coping, or do they just sit the moods out?

What are your expectations?

In asking this question, a therapist pays homage to the fact that the client should receive their money's worth. This is the chance for the client to express what they expect of the therapy. Clients always take particular interest in varied things. Some of them are more interested in homework, others in venting, and yet others in having a high level of interaction. A client's expectations allow the therapist to understand whether they are up to the task or not, whether they are dealing with a mentally stable person or some fantasist who lives in a bubble.

What would it take to make you feel more satisfied and happier?

The therapist gets the client to confirm their happiness on a scale of one to ten. They want to know how their client processes the world, what they dislike about people, what frustrates them, and how they handle these frustrations. Do they get mad when they fail to get their way? What changes would make them happy?

Do you have a low, average, or high interpersonal IQ?

This question is aimed at establishing whether the client is successful on the part of developing meaningful relationships with other people. How does society view them? Do they have a life partner? How cohesive is their family? What are their weaknesses in the context of functioning within a society?

Chapter 24: Developing a Therapeutic Relationship

The following are the critical elements of a successful therapeutic relationship:

Be skilled and experienced

Before anything else, a therapist must be skilled and experienced. The last thing any client wants is to encounter a therapist who hardly knows what they are doing. It would not only reflect badly on the individual therapist but also on the entire industry. Thankfully, the regulatory bodies do a wonderful job of ensuring that most therapists in practice are qualified, and have the appropriate licenses. However, just because the governing bodies are awake doesn't mean that there aren't a few rotten eggs trying to spoil things for everyone else. Beyond having the skills and the experience, a therapist must continue to replenish their knowledge through reading books and being interested in the current affairs touching upon CBT programs.

Build trust

A client is expected to be as honest as can be to get to the bottom of their problem. But the most critical element for a client to be open is trust. If a client senses that their therapist cannot be trusted, then they are going to clam up and keep some details hidden. To encourage your clients to trust you, you have to have an open approach. Clients are clever too. They can spot fake people from a mile off. However, if you show that you are an open therapist, that you are interested in helping the client get started on the path to full recovery, you will have given them enough push to be honest and sincere. But then, a therapist owes their client one thing: secrecy. Under no circumstances should a therapist divulge what their client had told them.

Show empathy

Let's say you're battling a major episode of depression which you believe is being fueled by your failing marriage. You log on to the internet and get the name of a therapist who administers CBT programs in town. Then you drive to their practice and seek an audience with them. Everything is fine until you started talking about your problem. As you launch into the gory details of how your husband insults you and all his babyish tendencies irk you, the therapist, seated across from you, starts laughing. Okay, you want to be mad at them, but wait, this is the therapist! You don't get mad at your therapist. However, this therapist clearly lacks empathy, and it's a wonder how they have survived in such an industry.

Give the client power

The therapist must not exhibit the tendencies of a dictator, i.e., holding all the power. They should devolve most of the activities to the client and take the position of the overseer. The client is not a small child who must be tracked every second. Besides, when you give your client the power, it makes them feel as though they are in control of their lives, which is a critical element at the psychological level.

Regulate the sessions

In as much as it is important to let the client dictate the things that they want, you are the principal. So you have to regulate the pace of the sessions. If the client goes much too fast, you should be there to slow them down, and conversely, if the client moves at an incredibly slow pace, you should make them move fast. When you are regulating the sessions, it sends the message that you are the one in control. This will ensure that the client not only respects you but looks up to you for guidance.

Enhance client skills and strengths

The job of a therapist is to find out the various strengths of their client. Once they find about these strengths, they should make a point of capitalizing on them, so that the client might improve their situation on the whole. The therapist must ensure that the client has coping skills and emotion regulation skills. As the client goes through various stages of recovery, they will run into tough emotional situations, and it will take their coping skills to overcome their challenges.

Address potential therapeutic barriers

There are many kinds of things that may act as barriers to effective therapy sessions. These challenges are both of a physical and psychological nature. Enlighten your client on some of these challenges so that they are not helpless. For instance, weird beliefs, delusions or voices can deter a client from making progress. A therapist should point out these barriers, while being proactive, transparent, and fostering a collaborative spirit. The success of a program is down to the ability of both the client and the therapist to collaborate.

Build your client up – don't tear them down

Since your client has been vulnerable and opened up to you about their deep secrets, the least you can do is build them up, not tear them down. You can start by making them realize that their past choices are not mistakes. Whether they went to questionable therapists, or whether they got into activities that have degraded their quality of life, you must make them see the good in them at all times. Considering that you are in a position of influence, uttering bad or negative things about them would cause them heartache.

Show your clients some respect

You have got someone who trusts you with their deep secrets, gives you money to coach them, and hangs on your every word, the least you could do is to show them major respect. Your respect should be natural. Not forced. If you find yourself having to fake it, then you must have a terrible disconnection with your client, which is a sign that you're not good in your job, considering that therapists have an innate potential of connecting with nearly anyone – actually, everyone.

Chapter 25: Common Errors Made in CBT

Not understanding the necessity of repetition for change

The key to successful cognitive therapy is a repetition of the statement that challenges erroneous thought patterns. The therapist must also use a tool that helps them achieve this. People don't alter their thinking patterns just because they have been told to do it. If that had been even remotely possible, then there'd be no need of CBT, considering that all it would take was hearing the right words, and then voila! The value of repetition cannot be emphasized in the effectiveness of CBT. This is also true for any new skill. Changing your thinking pattern is akin to acquiring a new skill. This shouldn't be misconstrued to mean that people have to be obsessed in their pursuit to alter their ways of thinking through CBT programs. To get the most out of CBT techniques, you must incorporate the techniques in your daily life, and eventually, you will manage to uproot your negative thought patterns and give way to a wholesome, new being, driven by thoughts of positivity.

Making assumptions about CBT based on social comparison

There are too many assumptions being made about CBT. However, what most of these people fail to recognize is that success doesn't happen on its own, and more importantly, that the CBT program is based on ideologies that seem natural. For most people who are successful – athletes, politicians, musicians, actors, painters, etc. – they must have learned these techniques naturally and assimilated them into their lives.

So, never assume that since you are studying these techniques and applying them on purpose, other people never have to go through that. You must understand that CBT techniques can be taken up by anyone in a natural setting, and these techniques would end up making all the difference.

Not making CBT techniques a lifestyle change

Many people make the mistake of approaching CBT as some form of treatment that may be endured for only a short amount of time. CBT is really about training your brain to give entirely new reactions and stay aligned to a positive mindset. Correcting an error in thinking a few times, and practicing CBT techniques for just enough time to witness a positive change is not useful. To enjoy the full benefits of CBT, people must view CBT as a total lifestyle change, something to be done on the regular.

Not using relaxation regularly

Some people expect to benefit from relaxation despite using it quite infrequently. Relaxation helps a person let go of their mental and physical strain. Sadly, people don't seem keen on maximizing on this practice. Relaxation is one of the easiest stress-free techniques to pull off; it remains a wonder why people are less inclined to pursue it. This technique can be used to condition the body to react differently, but still, this technique has a potential outcome. Our bodies can become conditioned to various stresses, and associate the stress to certain stimuli. For instance, people or events. Relaxation can help overcome such stresses, but to witness significant changes, it must be carried out regularly.

Expecting results without practice

Unlike what many people think, cognitive behavioral therapy is not a quick fix. If you're not going to be fully committed to the activities and processes, you had better stay away altogether. When you take on the techniques halfheartedly, you will not achieve any tangible results. You have to have some consistency. Depending on the needs and personality of the patient, the therapist will always tailor the CBT program to cater to them. But it is upon the client to work hard and incorporate CBT into their lives.

Believing that CBT is similar to positive thinking

Although CBT is aimed at converting a person from being a sufferer of negative thought patterns into being a person filled with positivity, you cannot use CBT and positive thinking interchangeably. The feelings of a person are closely related to their thoughts. Thus, by accessing a person's thoughts and applying some modifications, that person may be able to alter their feelings. In this way, CBT is perhaps the biggest tool that there is for banishing negativity and boosting the power of positivity. Positive thinking, on the other hand, is a learned behavior. This behavior promotes positivity too, but it's not as effective as CBT.

Believing emotions are always irrational

We are emotional beings. The decisions we make or don't make are guided by emotion. Emotions are involved in almost every aspect of our lives. It is impossible for us to get rid of our emotions, and we would be at a great disadvantage even if we did. For instance, our emotions are critical in alerting us to potential dangers, drawing our attention to a favorite person of the opposite sex, and giving us the courage to keep going. Sometimes, our emotions are inaccurate, but we shouldn't let this negate the important role that our emotions play.

Placing demands on mindfulness

Another error that people commonly make is placing demands on mindfulness. They fail to realize that placing demands on mindfulness will eliminate the benefits of mindfulness. Mindfulness is about letting yourself live in the present moment to the largest extent possible. For this reason, a person who's big on mindfulness is never influenced by material possessions or the pursuit of vanity. Thus, when you place your demands on mindfulness, you deny yourself the chance to practice mindfulness in an intended way.

Using CBT to justify not being responsible for a change

An incredible amount of money has been poured into the research for finding out the effectiveness of CBT. It was found that there are extremely high chances of recovery once patients take up this practice. Still, many people are somehow incapable of making any significant change in their lives, and they end up rubbishing the tools that are long proven as effective.

Chapter 26: DBT and ACT Tools and Techniques

Dialectical behavior therapy (DBT) is a type of cognitive behavioral therapy that emphasizes collaboration, support of the patient, and the cultivation of skills required to handle charged emotional situations. This treatment was originally tailored for people who struggle with suicidal thoughts, but it came to encompass a broad range of other conditions that involve dysfunctional emotional regulation.

There are two broad categories of dialectical behavior therapy:

- o Individual weekly therapy sessions
- o Weekly group therapy sessions

The following are some of the essential DBT skills and techniques to master:

Objectiveness effectiveness skills

- *Describe:* this explains your capacity to capture your internal feelings. The patient must find the right words that capture exactly how they feel. DBT awakens a patient to their true feelings. The more a patient can explain what ails them, the more they are likely to receive help.

• *Express:* a patient should be in a position to express their needs and wants. If they have an idea about how to improve their situation, then, by all means, they should express their idea, and ensure that they make the best use of the resources handed down to them.

• *Assert:* the DBT therapy teaches patients to wield some power and don't seem like victims. Their power can be seen in their assertiveness. Being an assertive person doesn't mean that one is aggressive or boastful, but it is merely a way of expressing their needs and standing their ground.

• *Reinforce:* no matter how great your ideas or plans might be, you will always need some form of reinforcement to actualize your plans. Knowing this, a patient should approach every challenge knowing that they will have to reinforce their ideas before they achieve whatever they set out for.

• *Mindful:* this skill restores a patient's focus to their present moment. Instead of letting their minds wander, pondering about the various things they have been engaged in or disengaged from, a patient should learn to have laser focus. This is a very critical element in the struggle against emotional health problems.

• *Confidence:* it is critical to have a high level of self-esteem. Being confident in yourself won't make you capable of moving mountains, but it will equip you with a positive mindset, which is a tremendous advantage. The more confident you are, the more you are likely to draw favorable circumstances to your life and make progress.

• *Negotiate:* DBT empowers a patient to learn of their power. They can challenge the existing order or way of doing things. Thus, a patient should try to negotiate terms, seeking ways that are favorable to them. When they are successful at establishing new terms, while banking on their power of negotiating, it can give their self-esteem a boost.

Relationship effectiveness skills

- *Gentle:* DBT teaches a patient to be gentle with their partner. Their partner would be more receptive of them if they took a gentle approach. However, if they are rough and pay no attention to how they handle their partner, then there are going to be a whole lot of problems.
- *Interested:* DBT emphasizes showing interest, and not merely hoping that your partner will understand you value them. Partners are incredibly sensitive to the little things that are done or not done, and this can mean a huge difference between the success and failure of a relationship.
- *Validate:* the idea that we don't need validation is kind of flawed. The truth is that we are in need of validation from the people we consider important. Our relationship partners are important enough, and their validation means a lot. But then, just as you seek validation from your spouse, you must return the favor, lest it becomes a toxic arrangement.

Self-respect effectiveness skills

- *Fair:* at all times, one must seek to practice fairness. This means you must be fair to others, but more importantly, you must be fair to yourself. Never let others have their way at your expense. If you don't care about yourself, no one else will. Being fair is a step in the right direction.
- *Apologies:* you are going to have unpleasant encounters with people. If you're in the wrong, you must offer an

apology, and if you're wronged, you should solicit an apology. A solicited apology is not the best, but it shows that the aggressor has goodwill.

- *Truthful:* saying the truth is the one thing that you owe yourself and the world alike. It is not a very common thing, but there's no harm to it. Furthermore, it simplifies your life.

When it comes to acceptance and commitment therapy (ACT), the goal is to increase psychological flexibility and establish more focus to the present.

The following are some of the principles of the ACT:

Acceptance

Each person struggles with their negative thoughts. Their instinctive reaction is to try to suppress these thoughts, but is it worth it? ACT teaches patients to accept their negative thoughts. They have to make room for unpleasant feelings, urges, and sensations. The apparent abundance mindset makes it easier to get rid of the negative things that you have always taken an interest in.

Cognitive defusion

This entails perceiving thoughts, words, images, and other cognitive activities in a standalone sense. They are to mean the exact thing that they stand for and must not be pieced together to form a bigger idea. It is the opposite of what is known as cognitive fusion, which seeks to "fuse" various cognitions and form a large mental product. For instance, the mere words, "chocolate-cake" are enough to have us drooling as they plant the image of the cake in our minds. Patients may use cognitive defusion to not pay great meaning to the images and languages that pop up in their minds.

Chapter 27: How Long Does It Take for CBT to Work?

One of the advantages of CBT is its ability to tackle symptoms in a short span, typically from a few weeks to a few months. It is widely held that the results of CBT start to come out within eight to twelve weeks of therapy. The average person seeking CBT therapy might have more than one area to work on, and such a person will take longer to achieve full results. The most definitive answer to the question about how long it takes for CBT to bear fruit is that it depends. CBT aims at striking at a patient's fears repeatedly until they are forced to shape up.

The following are some of the aspects that have an impact on the length of CBT treatment:

A client's lack of basic skills

When a client meets up with a therapist to embark on CBT program, both of them must work together to realize their goals. There are some basic skills that the client ought to have; for instance, the ability to self-soothe to reduce anxiety, as well as make the right decisions. When a client is lacking in this department, the things that would have been a breeze getting through become a complex affair, and both the client and the therapist are forced to be dragged along. The more there are such cases, the more time will be wasted.

Previous negative experiences with mental health care

If a client is not new to CBT treatment, the chances are that they have worked with other therapists before, either to solve what ails them at present or their past illnesses. If the client had a negative experience with a therapist from the past, then it might affect their relationship with future therapists.

The following are some factors that might have contributed to the falling out:

> • *The therapy didn't help at all:* in other words, the client was of the mind that they had thrown their money away. If a therapy fails to achieve results, let alone the desired results, it can leave a bitter taste in the client's mouth. Depending on the kind of therapy that the client had sought, it may have cost them a figurative arm and a leg. Now holding their zero achievements next to the money that they had pumped into the practice will leave the client feeling gutted. Moving on, the client becomes wary of therapists, and this seeming tinge of suspicion can underwhelm the therapist and slow things down.
>
> • *Disagreements with the therapist:* every client has their own set of unique traits. Some of the clients are humble and easy to get along with, whereas others are combative hell-raisers. They question everything and even try to challenge the smartness of the therapist. If a hell-raising client found out something in the program that they disagreed with, they would make no compromises. They would express their disgust and stand their ground. The therapist would be hard pressed to tweak the program to suit the needs of their client, even though they knew too

well that the previous arrangement would have achieved the best results.

- *Financial troubles:* CBT treatment is relatively affordable when you put other methods of treatment into the equation. Depending on the payment methods that clients choose, some clients exhibit parasitic tendencies, and they want to receive their treatment, even though they are not willing or ready or able to pay the full amount. They are the classic self-entitled types who have no respect for other people's time. Basic decency denotes that you should agree with your therapist on your payment arrangements and you must keep your word. If for some reason you are unable to raise funds, then you should stay away until you can afford. In as much as the client wants to receive treatment, they must also understand that the therapist is in business, and not an all-altruistic healer with a billion-dollar fortune.

Fear of change

CBT incorporates techniques that can shake up a person's normal lifestyle. For a client who's scared of facing change, they present an incredible challenge to their therapist. Their fear of change acts as a psychological impediment. When a client is not enthusiastic about taking the various steps of CBT treatment, they lessen their capacity to achieve the full benefits of the CBT program. And this can make the treatment drag for much longer than necessary.

Lack of motivation

When a client lacks motivation, they limit their capacity of reaching their goals. A lack of motivation can be seen in their cavalier approach to the program, continuous failure to complete their homework, a sense of entitlement, and in extreme cases, looking down upon their therapist. All of these not only contribute toward slowing down the program but also cheapening their results.

Inexperienced therapist

A therapist might be theoretically qualified to take on various clients, but still, they lack the depth and capacity to handle the problem. Some clients have such complicated issues that they require an 'old hand'. When a therapist is inexperienced, they never let the client know, but it shows in their behaviors.

Poor leadership skills

The therapist is the leader, and the client is the follower, and that's how it should remain. However, some therapists have such poor leadership skills that they are unable to bring the client onto the same page as them, and this uneasiness is a general hindrance to the success of the program.

High levels of pressure or stress caused by poor living standards

When a client operates from a stressed point, it means that they are not in a position to utilize their brain to the maximum, which will obviously lower the results they achieve with CBT.

Discouragement from friends and family

CBT may be a remarkably effective mode of treatment, but it is still not widely practiced. Some people have what we call "mixed feelings" about CBT. Clients may be discouraged by their friends and family from taking CBT and opting for a "proper" treatment, which obviously weighs down their psyche.

Chapter 28: Ways to Lighten Up When You're Down

Life's challenges can cause you to become overwhelmed. Being cast down comes with a feeling of invisibility and subjugation. But life was meant to be enjoyed.

The following tips will help you take a lighter approach to life:

Let go of your expectations

Nothing depresses a person quicker than having their expectations shattered. If you set lofty expectations for yourself, you are needlessly putting yourself in harm's way. Have goals, but get rid of expectations. Such a mindset will increase your focus, and you will become less hurt by terrible outcomes.

Avoid stressful situations

Stress is one of the main factors that will stop you from having a light mood. To get rid of stress, you must avoid situations that activate your stress. For instance, if arguing with your spouse leaves you stressed, make a conscious effort to not argue with them.

Release your tension

When you are holding a lot of tension inside of you, you can become incapable of having a light mood. Let go of your tension by engaging in things like exercise and having fun. When you eliminate tension from your body and mind, you will get into the right mood.

Limit negativity

Negative thoughts breed negative feelings and actions. When you nurse negativity, you become incapable of experiencing life through a joyful perspective. To give room to positivity, start by avoiding the things that trigger your negative reactions. For instance, it could be watching violent films, or hanging around toxic people.

Forgive

This approach is two-pronged. You have to forgive yourself and others too. Stop holding grudges against people who slighted you. And stop dwelling on your limitations. When you have forgiven yourself and others, you will enter a positive frame of mind, which will allow you to experience the joy of a child.

Limit or get rid of negative people from your life

The friends that you keep will influence your habits and mindset. If there are negative people in your life, that is the energy you don't need. Try to limit the time you spend with them or eliminate them from your life altogether.

Bend the rules

Don't take this as a free pass to becoming a criminal. There's a huge difference between bending the rules and breaking them. Bending the rules means that living on the edge doesn't particularly scare you. It will make you seem fascinating and draw people toward you.

Never give up

Your mindset should be: "No challenge is too big for me!" If this is your mindset, you will never stop improving yourself. You will always have the energy to go the extra mile. By never giving up, you position yourself to achieve tremendous success.

Have a sense of humor

Are you the kind of person who will think back to a time you had embarrassed yourself and start laughing? If you're that person, it means that you have a sense of humor. Ensure that you've replaced your sensitivity and embarrassment with a sense of humor.

Always see the positive side

You should view your glass as half filled, not half empty. This mindset is critical in always noticing the bright side of things. No matter how awful an experience first seems, there's still something positive to it. All you have to do is look hard enough.

Increase your circle of positive friends

Just because you eliminated the bad ones from your circle doesn't mean you're not interested in making friends. You sure are. However, you're interested in making friends with positive people. If you meet a person who exudes positivity, you might want to make them your friend.

Meditate

Ensure that you meditate every day. At the appointed time, just retreat to your place of seclusion, and get into your meditation. Meditation is a great way of clearing the noise from your mind and setting you up for a joy-filled mood.

Proper posture

When you sit down or when you stand, always keep an erect posture, never slouch. This sends the message to others that you know what you're doing – you're full of confidence. But if you take up a small space, slouch, and try to look small, people will pick up on your inferiority.

Travel

The next moment you are feeling down, just hop onto a train and travel as far away as you can. The change in environment and the meeting of new people will surely put you into a celebratory mood. Traveling is one of those things that lightens up your mood effortlessly.

Get into your hobby

Maybe you have been getting depressed because of losing yourself in your office job and forgetting that you have other passions. What are your hobbies? Doing something that you genuinely love is going to lighten you up and fill you up with a childlike sense of wonder.

Spend time in nature

Have you been spending a lot of your time inside small white-walled offices and are on the verge of losing it? Your remedy is nothing complex: just spend a few hours in nature. The trees, flowers, and landscapes will give you a little of their awesomeness.

Practice mindfulness

Always be fully present. When you have a wandering mind, your mental energy will be depleted much too soon. You will keep scrutinizing past events, albeit unconsciously, and end up draining your energy. Keep your full attention to the task at hand, regardless of whether it is a serious activity, such as banking your money, or a less serious one, such as taking a bathroom break. When you practice mindfulness, you will always seem to have enough energy to live in the present.

Lavishing your favorite pet with attention can do wonders to your mood too. Pets are genuine little creatures, and they teach us to be grateful and enjoy life.

Chapter 29: Myths and Misconceptions

Myth: CBT neglects to address past behavior

For a therapist to create a program that will suit the needs of their client, they have to first understand where the client is coming from. This can only be achieved by questioning their past. Although CBT doesn't directly treat past traumas, the affected person is empowered in the sense that they can now put a timeline to the history of their emotional troubles. Additionally, CBT helps a person unlearn false beliefs, which they had obviously picked up in the past.

Myth: CBT is too scientific and rigid in its practice

Although CBT has a very scientific background, its application isn't steeped in too much science. Actually, even a grandmother can receive CBT programs without a glitch. A therapist will seek to establish the thought patterns behind a certain feeling or behavior, and then use data analysis systems to come up with the right criteria for modifying their client's thoughts. In CBT techniques, the therapist's scientific mind is enough, but in its application, everything is free-flowing. Besides, it takes the therapist and the client to work out a program that satisfies the needs of the client.

Myth: CBT neglects the client and therapist relationship

If the client and the therapist have no close relationship, no progress can be made. You realize that CBT requires the client to become vulnerable and to open up about possibly their darkest secrets unknown to nobody else. Is it possible for that to take place if the client and the therapist hadn't shared close ties? In some techniques, the therapist and the client will share intimate space, and it can only be aided by the fact that they are in good terms. Nothing would destroy CBT faster than a messy client-therapist relationship.

Myth: CBT only treats symptoms, not people

The truth is that CBT tackles both the symptoms and the sufferer. In as much as tackling the symptoms is critical to the success of CBT, the best results involve treating the patient fully. By focusing on the dysfunctional problems and emotional loops that have contributed to the sufferer living through painful experiences, CBT surely caters to the affected person, just as much if not more, than their symptoms. However, this is easy to miss because much of the effort is seen as undue attention on the symptoms, forgetting that these CBT hacks are designed to go around and modify the person as a whole. CBT tracks down the thought patterns that contribute to the feelings of a person, and whether or not the person will question how their lifestyle correlates with their cognitive activities is a matter of personal choice. For instance, through CBT, the negative thoughts that a person holds will be exposed as responsible for the terrible moods that the person is struggling with. It is upon that person to be introspective and find out which circumstances have led them into absorbing negativity. Maybe, they have a tendency of fighting with their spouse, or maybe the associates that they keep are pessimistic energy vampires. CBT promotes the growth of brain cells. Scientists have found out that as a person learns new things, their brain develops fresh neural connections, in a process known as neuroplasticity, as though it were creating more space for "data storage". Since CBT incorporates many techniques and principles, the brain is subjected to an intense learning phase, and more neural connections are made neural, and the overall brain health of the individual is given a boost.

CBT requires clients to be motivated

Not every patient that a therapist receives will be motivated to practice the various CBT techniques. Some patients will have zero motivation. The therapist may work jointly with them to set a goal that will hopefully motivate them. The therapist takes it as their primary responsibility to get the client to be motivated, but they can only try so hard. For instance, they may prod into the client's past, seeking to understand the reasons behind the total loss of motivation, and then provide a remedy. The client may keep a record of their motivation statuses in a journal.

CBT is a superficial pseudoscience

CBT is neither a pseudoscience nor is it superficial. To understand a person's actions and emotions, you would have to go through the route of thought. The thoughts that a person holds are interconnected with their behaviors and emotions. Thus, learning a person's thoughts gives you insight into their behaviors, and the causes of those undesirable thoughts, which in most cases are past traumatic events. For a person who is only beginning to learn about the complex relationship between their mind, emotions, and actions, CBT can be an extremely challenging practice.

There are no obvious ways of telling whether the therapy has worked

If you held such a myth, then it would mean that the millions of people around the world seeking CBT treatment are somehow deranged, considering that they will never get their money's worth. CBT is useful in treating a number of conditions. CBT is not guesswork. When this age-old practice first received backlash, scientists took an interest in it, and their findings shocked the world. CBT was found to be effective in treating a number of illnesses – particularly mental health illnesses – and the success rate was way above what conventional medicine had been posting. Considering that more research and more money are being committed to CBT, the future looks bright.

Conclusion

Cognitive behavioral therapy is a type of psychotherapy that helps a person to alter their behaviors and emotions by challenging their negative thinking patterns concerning themselves or the world.

The following are some of the critical tools and techniques employed in CBT:

Journaling: this technique is important in that it helps an individual understand the various thoughts and emotions they experience in a day.

Unraveling cognitive distortions: generally, there are some thoughts that we hold that are untrue and mislead us. This technique helps us uncover such fallacies.

Cognitive restructuring: once we discover the various distorted thoughts that we hold, we can begin investigating the root cause of these problems, and it helps us get rid of our unhelpful thoughts.

Exposure and response prevention: in the case of OCD sufferers, they can overcome their compulsions not by running away from them but by exposing themselves to their fears.

Nightmare exposure and rescripting: for some of us who have trouble overcoming our fear of the dark, this technique helps us confront our fear in a controlled environment, so that we may gain power over it.

Progressive music relaxation: they say music is life, and yet music plays a critical role in helping us get rid of our fears, and become well-balanced individuals.

Relaxed breathing: this technique is aimed at eliminating the noise from our mind and heightening our awareness. To practice relaxed breathing, all we have to do is look for a serene environment, and perform deep-breathing exercises.

Check out more books by Steven Turner

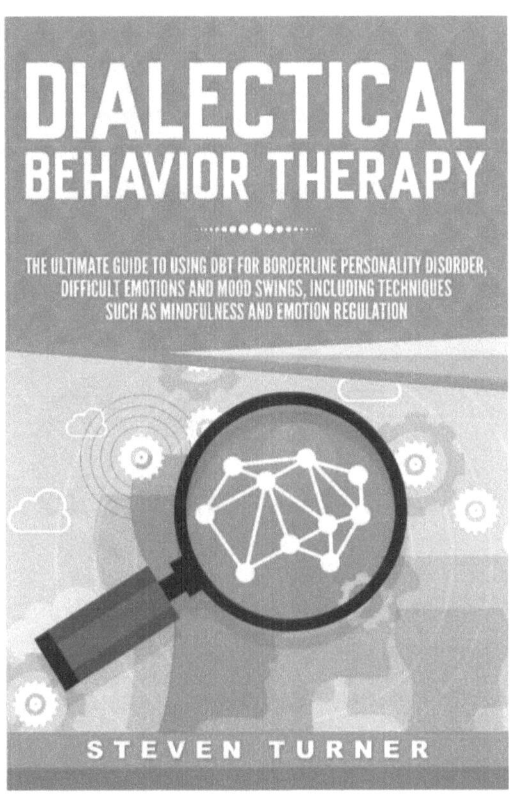

EMOTIONAL INTELLIGENCE
HOW TO BOOST YOUR EQ, IMPROVE SOCIAL SKILLS, SELF-AWARENESS, LEADERSHIP SKILLS, RELATIONSHIPS, CHARISMA, SELF-DISCIPLINE, BECOME AN EMPATH, LEARN NLP AND ACHIEVE SUCCESS
STEVEN TURNER

EMPATH
Your Guide to Understanding Empaths and
Their Emotional Abilities to Feel Empathy,
Including Tips for Highly Sensitive People, Dealing
with Energy Vampires, and Being a Psychic Empath
Steven Turner

DARK
PSYCHOLOGY
What Machiavellian People of Power Know
about Persuasion, Mind Control, Manipulation,
Negotiation, Deception, Human Behavior,
and Psychological Warfare that You Don't
Steven Turner